Praise

"Dr. Stephen S. Tang's *A Test for Our Time* is a must-read for anyone looking to lead with empathy and courage in a time of crisis. His inspiring story will surely help readers around the world take on any challenge with confidence and resilience."—Vincent A. Forlenza, Retired Chairman, BD (Becton, Dickinson and Company)

"Steve Tang is an extraordinary leader who, through his story in *A Test for Our Time*, inspires business leaders to lead wholeheartedly and rise to the challenge of a crisis. As a CEO myself during the COVID crisis, I can attest to the authenticity of Steve's struggles and courage. This remarkable story is valuable for its self-awareness about transformation as a leader and practical lessons distilled from that crucible experience." —Eric Schurenberg, Editor in Chief, Amplify Publishing Group, Former CEO and Editor in Chief, *Inc.* and *Fast Company*

"This book offers helpful lessons that can help leaders prepare for the next crisis. Everyone should read it and take its advice seriously. "—Richard W. Vague, Founder, Tychos, author of *A Brief History of Doom* and *The Next Economic Disaster*

"Steve Tang 's compelling inside story of guiding a company through an unexpected upheaval, is both inspiring and full of helpful insights. The aspiring executive and leader can learn and apply his lessons."—Alex Liu, Managing Partner & Chairman, Kearney, author of *Joy Works*

"A Test for Our Time is a powerful reminder that no matter how bleak things may seem, we all have the capacity to overcome any obstacle. Dr. Tang's inspiring story will undoubtedly motivate and guide leaders around the world."—Melissa L. Bradley, Founder & CEO, 1863 Ventures

"Trust is a magical force that gives us the courage to move forward, even in the face of adversity. A Test for Our Time provides invaluable insight on how to lead with your whole heart so people can trust you and bring their best selves to the team. It is an essential read for anyone who wants to become a better leader."—Esther Baldwin, Artificial Intelligence Strategist, Architect, Intel Corporation, Eisenhower Fellow

"*A Test for Our Time* is an invaluable resource for leaders of any industry, providing readers with valuable lessons for navigating a crisis. Dr. Tang's remarkable story and words of wisdom will certainly inspire readers around the world."—Victor W. Hwang, Founder & CEO, Right to Start, co-author of *The Rainforest: The Secret to Building the Next Silicon Valley*

"*A Test for Our Time* provides a unique insight into the power of resilience, courage and self-discovery during difficult times. Dr. Tang's incredible journey will surely serve as an inspiration and beacon for leaders around the globe."—Jay H. Shah, Executive Chairman, Hersha Hotels & Resorts

"Steve Tang's *A Test for Our Time* brings the essentials of leading through crisis to life, highlighting practical and pragmatic elements every leader must master to succeed. As we anticipate and prepare for future disruptions, these human lessons will be invaluable in navigating turbulent times. With the storyteller's skill and insight, Tang provides readers with an authoritative guide for thriving during a crisis."—Karl Hofmann, President & CEO, Population Services International

"Dr. Tang's inspiring story in *A Test for Our Time* is sure to help readers everywhere take on any challenge with determination and resilience. His remarkable account is an invaluable guide to leading through adversity."—Anthony S. Bartolomeo, retired President & CEO, Pennoni Associates

"*A Test for Our Time* is a must-have on any leader's bookshelf. Dr. Tang has written an incredibly inspiring story of crisis leadership that will provide readers with valuable lessons for the future."—Maribel Perez Wadsworth, former President, Gannett Media

"Steve Tang's success is a testament to his unwavering commitment to excellence and innovation. At OraSure, he created an incredible culture of trust, respect, and collaboration that has allowed his team to thrive in an unprecedented time. His dedication and passion for his work is an inspiration for us all!"—Dr. Matthew T. Lambert, CEO, William & Mary Foundation

"An uplifting narrative of leadership during some of the most turbulent times of our generation, illuminated by the wisdom of acclaimed authors Adam Grant, Simon Sinek, Bill George, Brené Brown and more."—Tiffany Wilson, President & CEO, University City Science Center

"Steve Tang helped us build an innovative culture where everyone can be heard and ideas can be shared. He's been an inspirational role model to me for leadership and mentorship. All will learn from this book."—Lisa Nibauer, former President, Diagnostics, OraSure Technologies Inc.

"As CEO, Steve Tang's passion for innovation was contagious, and his determination was inspiring. He also placed enormous trust in us, which led to all to succeed."—Dr. Jody D. Berry, former Chief Scientific Officer, Diagnostics, OraSure Technologies Inc.

"Dr. Tang's dedication to communication and alignment during difficult times was admirable, as was his focus on diversity, equity, and inclusion. He genuinely cared about the well-being of his team. He has left a lasting legacy in this book!"—Jose Rosado, former Vice President, Quality, OraSure Technologies Inc.

A TEST FOR OUR TIME

A TEST FOR OUR TIME

CRISIS LEADERSHIP IN THE NEXT NORMAL

Dear Bill,

Thank you for your support, encouragement, and keyrole you've played in this story?

Energy, love, +

lead wholeheartedly!

STEPHEN S. TANG

NEW DEGREE PRESS

A TEST FOR OUR TIME
Crisis Leadership in the Next Normal

ISBN   979-8-88926-900-7   *Paperback*
         979-8-88926-902-1   *Hardcover*
         979-8-88926-901-4   *Ebook*

Dedication

———

To my loving family, past, present, and future...

Jill...

Lauren, Rob, Remi, Nico...

Beau...

Helana...

Helen and Walter...

To all who have journeyed as immigrants, refugees, and entrepreneurs... especially my grandparents.

To all who have journeyed within themselves, faced and overcome pain and prejudice, and created their own privilege.

To anyone on those journeys... I see you, hear you, and love your courage.

Contents

Introduction: Excavator

"Sometimes it is the people who no one imagines anything of who do the things that no one can imagine."

—JOAN CLARKE TO ALAN TURING, COMPUTER
SCIENCE AND ARTIFICIAL INTELLIGENCE
PIONEER, IN *THE IMITATION GAME*

On March 23, 2021, the colossal container ship *Ever Given* ran aground in the Suez Canal, blocking traffic and disrupting global supply chains. Carrying a staggering eighteen thousand containers, the vessel was one of the largest in the world, making it all the more impactful when it came to a halt. The canal is a key artery for global trade. Around 12 percent of international commerce passes through each year. So, this blockage caused major delays and implications for businesses worldwide. Experts estimated it could take weeks before traffic returned to normal as crews scrambled to clear out the obstruction. Like the beginning of the coronavirus pandemic a year before, one seemingly small incident can reverberate far beyond what we might expect.

When Abdullah Abdul-Gawad took on the task of freeing the *Ever Given* from its rock and mud entrapment, he probably couldn't have imagined that a meme would later capture his humble excavator's efforts. In this now widely circulated image, it appeared as though Abdul-Gawad's minuscule machine is trying to tackle a seemingly insurmountable task—attempting to pry apart the colossal vessel with what looks like an almost comically small tool. This meme took on a life of its own, often being used in situations where someone is facing an impossible challenge or when hope seems lost. Abdul-Gawad's story serves as a testament to persevering in the face of overwhelming odds.

As Mia Jankowicz reported for *Business Insider* (Jankowicz 2021), Abdul-Gawad felt as if "everyone was just making fun of it . . . And that was what made me so determined," he continued. "I was like, you know, you're making fun of me. So, I'm absolutely going to prove that I can do this." But it was by no means clear he could. It was a precarious situation because there was the risk that the ship could capsize as it was being dislodged and crush the excavator and Abdul-Gawad.

"It can't really be funny to me because I didn't know whether this ship was going to come out or not, and I was in the middle of the situation," he said. It became a personal mission. As the days wore on, Abdul-Gawad said he and his colleagues grabbed brief moments of rest in a barracks used by border guards working nearby. At most, he said they got about three hours of sleep a night, and one night, they took only one hour.

Two days later, a specialized dredger joined the efforts. Abdul-Gawad's job was to shift rock and sand from the ship's bow while the dredger dislodged the silt from the canal bed. The combined effort—with the help of a high tide—gave hopeful signs the next day, and they finally succeeded on March 29. *Ever Given*'s release set every Suez Canal worker cheering—and the world exulting—in celebration. Abdul-Gawad and his colleagues had been "half-dead with exhaustion. [They] had been stretched to [their] limit" (Sukheja 2021). Yet he was an afterthought in the official celebrations—invited an hour and a half before the festivities started, four hours of travel away from him.

This six-day drama became a triumphant underdog story within the carnage and devastation of the coronavirus pandemic. In it, Abdullah Abdul-Gawad went from an unknown twenty-eight-year-old to social media ridicule to unsung hero. Other stories like his have yet to be told. Here is one of them.

Amid a global pandemic, one small company stepped up to fight the contagion head-on. This is the story of their journey—from the everyday people who did the extraordinary to the leaders who inspired them to achieve great things. Sometimes it felt like space exploration with all its pioneering spirit and inherent danger. Other times, it was like *The Twilight Zone*, impossible to predict what would happen next. And at other times, it was like *Alice in Wonderland*, bizarre, disorienting, and threatening.

I was fortunate to be on the team at OraSure Technologies, Inc., a company that created the acclaimed InteliSwab Rapid COVID-19 Test. Proclaimed as the "easiest to use" test of its kind and the "#1 Standout Product" to hit drug store shelves in 2021, InteliSwab is truly a test for our time! Somehow, it seemed to be my career's destiny to be there.

Twice blessed, I was OraSure's chief executive officer through it all. We were an underdog company with an understated leader—all destined to live, learn, survive, and thrive together. No one on Earth was adequately prepared to deal with the coronavirus and its insidious menace, especially the world's leaders. If luck favors the prepared, we weren't lucky at all. The next best fate was to be fast learners about the crisis and act with compassion, empowerment, and accountability. Together, we were able to navigate these uncharted waters and come out stronger on the other side… from the "new normal" into the "next normal." How are they different? The "new normal" is the current reality, while the "next normal" is a vision for what our post-pandemic world could look like if we act on the lessons learned from life with the coronavirus. Our "next normal" is a chance for us to make lasting changes and build a better future.

Crisis leadership is like captaining a huge ship through choppy waters and an excavator operator who saves the day. In both cases, it takes a cool head, decisive action, and steady nerves to ensure the safety of people and property. But that's not all. Compassion is essential too, offering warmth in troubled times. Empowerment provides illumination along the way, and accountability serves as a ballast of trust when everything else is uncertain. When these qualities come together, they form a powerful force capable of guiding us through even the most turbulent storms with stamina.

In the next normal, our resilience will be tested by more than just COVID-19, Ebola, and Mpox. Our next normal won't be the pre-pandemic normal or what we think is normal today. The next normal will be an ever-changing period of adjustment for us all. As climate change disrupts animal eco-systems, viruses capable of crossing species boundaries seem increasingly inevitable to trigger other pandemics. Moreover, extreme weather events, social unrest, political instability, economic stagnation, and inequality alongside geopolitical power struggles all pose significant threats that can easily upend our most well-prepared plans. Only through a com-bination of preparedness and adaptability will we be able to survive in this new reality. Next normal is a reminder that no matter the unstable challenges we may face, there is always an opportunity to create a better future. By embracing the idea of the next normal, we can continue to progress and grow despite the many obstacles that come our way.

As we grapple with the ongoing realities of the pandemic, good leaders need to stay resilient and prepared for what-ever challenges may come their way. But that requires more than just a willingness to face uncertainty. It means *leading whole people wholeheartedly*—both now and in the next nor-mal. That means having an authentic connection with those you lead, demonstrating that you genuinely care about their well-being beyond simply expecting productive work from them. By cultivating meaningful relationships rooted in trust and understanding, we can continue pushing forward no matter what lies ahead. Let's make sure we don't let anything stop us from achieving our goals!

Wholehearted leaders are transparent about the severity of our plights and the decisions we make to address them. We support our team and infuse them with confidence in their ability to overcome obstacles because we hired them to do so. By leading whole people wholeheartedly, we can create strong teams capable of weathering any condition in the next normal.

Leading wholeheartedly requires an emotional connection through sincere expression. I've struggled with this for years, beginning with childhood as a shy, awkward kid of color. Thanks to the help of my coaches, psychotherapists, and wife (who is also a communications expert), I've made progress. I've found that writing is one of the best ways for me to express myself fully and authentically, which has been especially important during the pandemic when we couldn't be together in person. In April 2020, I started writing Monday Motivational Messages (MMMs) to help my OraSure colleagues stay connected and energized. Writing takes practice and vulnerability, but it's worth it because it purifies and clarifies our true intentions and allows us to lead from the heart.

As the pandemic continued, I found myself having more and more conversations with my employees about a whole range of topics—from family and music to humor, privilege, and prejudice. In these conversations, I offered my honesty about the everyday stress, anxiety, and uncertainty that came with the pandemic. I also addressed head-on the emotionally charged issues of religion, social injustice, and polarizing politics. I urged them to care for themselves, their families, loved ones, colleagues, and communities. I admitted that we were all in the same storm together but in different boats. And I was deeply concerned about each of their boats and sailors—especially those teams who continued to work in our factories and labs, as well as those nuclear and extended families who were living, working, and schooling in homes together twenty-four-seven.

As I sought to comfort them, they comforted me with their thoughtful responses to my weekly letters. Many shared that their partners' employers weren't communicating with employees at all, so my letters began to stand out by exception. Some let me know they were sharing my letters with their family and friends to help them cope with the twists and turns of the pandemic.

Between April 2020 and March 2022, my dialogue with employees resulted in two hundred and forty pages of correspondence. They felt more like "love letters" than company newsletters. In the coming pages, you'll see references to some of those letters. In the sections between chapters, you'll find a brief passage to me from my former OraSure colleagues (unnamed to protect the innocent) as glimpses of our ongoing dialogue. This story is about how OraSure triumphed during the pandemic, yet it translates well for leading in any foreseeable or unforeseeable crisis from here on. Along with the race to develop InteliSwab, we'll also explore my improbable journey to OraSure, the unique history of the company, how we first survived and then thrived together during the pandemic, and what we learned from it all. This book draws from mainstream business leadership but with a deeper focus on our shared human experience.

It's not all about glory, though. In the end, OraSure continued their journey without me. It was a sad departure for us all. And I share what I learned about that and my life beyond it. This book is a "I was in a tough spot and learned a lot" memoir chock full of lessons and advice for leaders, aspiring leaders, and those who love them—particularly those seeking new ways of inspiring and motivating people. I aim to raise the bar for effective crisis leadership by sharing with you how OraSure succeeded while I also share:

- My unorthodox career and life path that culminated in nearly four decades as a top executive who adapted to three major crises.
- The essence of trust, capability, opportunity, and strategy.
- How the unforeseen affects strategy.
- "Embracing the suck." Why physical, mental, emotional, and spiritual health beyond survival is imperative.
- How transformation is based on flourishing and collective effervescence.
- How shared stories foster deep and meaningful connection and engagement.
- How to say goodbye and leave "conditions for growth" as a legacy.
- The need for "wounded healers" to help each other.
- Leading whole people wholeheartedly as pastors and ancient dragomen.
- A call to action for better approaches to leading remote and hybrid workers.
- And how I dealt with setbacks and learned perspective for my life ahead.

The pandemic had us all in its grips, but some of us worked tirelessly to help others find freedom. We were reverent memes of Abdullah Abdul-Gawad clearing a blocked canal. With the creation of InteliSwab as proverbial excavators, a select few of us made it possible for many more to leave their confinement. Here is our story of rescue and redemption.

Dear Steve...

"I hope you can take your Monday Motivational Messages and morph them into a book or a good case study. Our company's journey in the last few years has been remarkable."

Prologue: Explorer

———

"I did not tell half of what I saw, for I knew I would not be believed."

—MARCO POLO, EXPLORER, MERCHANT, AND WRITER

"Are you sure you want to be the president and CEO of Ora-Sure?" That's what my wife, Jill, asked me a few months after we got married. By the time of the board meeting in August 2017, it was becoming clear I could be the next CEO of Ora-Sure. But many people close to me wondered whether I was making the right decision, taking on such a big challenge. I was confident in OraSure and its potential. And I believed that, with hard work and dedication, we could make it a great success.

Jill's question made sense. I didn't need to make a career change. For nearly ten years, I had been president and CEO of Philadelphia's University City Science Center. The Science Center had been founded in 1962, but its reputation had been badly tarnished before my arrival. Under my leadership, the

Science Center underwent a major transformation, becoming a world-class innovation hub. We expanded our campus with the addition of uCity Square—a one-billion-dollar mixed-use commercial real estate project—and attracted new businesses and entrepreneurs to our community. Today, the Science Center is still thriving.

Yet something about the OraSure opportunity was tugging at my mind and heart. Could a guy who explored uncharted worlds of innovation—like some latter-day Marco Polo—ignite discoveries and pathways in a company that desperately needed it? OraSure had some highly useful healthcare products that were profitable, but its product pipeline needed to be dramatically improved. As someone with experience in leading similar organizations and an advocate of life science entrepreneurship, I felt I could make a difference at OraSure.

Even so, Jill and I had just begun our new lives together (second marriages for both of us). She had just begun learning about my community at the Science Center. My commute to OraSure would absorb three to four hours every day, and she knew I would throw myself into the job from the get-go. All that would disrupt our cozy newlywed world. Months after I took the job, she tearfully confided to our marriage therapist that she didn't want me to make the change. We've since made peace about that decision and its effect on our relationship, but it took its toll for many years.

Both of us have since been amused to learn that the Obamas had a similar rift when Barack decided to run for president in 2008. When Barack first approached Michelle about his plan to run for president, she was not on board. She shot the idea down directly. However, eventually, she did change her mind, though she never fully forgave her husband for putting her and their daughters through the difficult campaign process. In a 2020 interview with Stephen Colbert, Barack explained his wife's initial reaction was "no . . . and she still remained mad at me for eight years [of my presidency], and there was still a little carryover for the next year and a half . . . and I think she finally forgave me" (Roberts 2020).

I can now relate to both his and her side of that incident. What lay ahead of Jill and me in 2018 was fated to be then unimaginable and draw us into a close "survive and thrive" partnership during many difficult times. As an executive leadership development coach and former Emmy Award-winning Philadelphia television reporter and news anchor, she knew of the daunting challenges ahead and held our best interests in her heart and soul. What Jill didn't know at the time was that my flirtation with OraSure began many years before my board service began in 2011 and had seduced me ever since.

HELLO, BETHLEHEM!

I arrived in Bethlehem, Pennsylvania, in August 1982 to begin graduate studies at Lehigh University. The city and Bethlehem Steel were declining due to fierce competition from steel "mini-mills" in Japan, Korea, and Germany. In front of the Bethlehem headquarters of the United Steel Workers of America, a hundred-foot steel I-beam was painted fire-engine red with the words "Stop Illegal Steel Imports" emblazoned in large white letters. Cars that entered the steel mill property were greeted with a sign that read, "Parking for American cars only. Park your Japanese car in Tokyo." Such was the edgy passive-aggressive mood of the region.

Martin Tower—home of BethSteel—became a cautionary example of corporate excess in business school case studies. The steel company's headquarters building was designed as a plus sign when viewed from above to create the maximum number of corner offices for senior executives. Crime was a problem in Southside Bethlehem, where the university, steel mill, and once-vibrant working-class neighborhoods were located. Lehigh students were warned to stay west of New Street for their safety.

I rented my first apartment in a Victorian home in what is now transitional housing for New Bethany Ministries. For two hundred seventy-five dollars per month, I had a bachelor pad, fully furnished with a sleigh bed and desk that was probably from the 1900s, a mid-century style kitchen, and a new Sears couch. The August heat meant the windows were always open. Without screens in them, I learned to chase away squirrels and birds who tried to become my roommates.

When I decided to pursue my master's and doctorate degrees in what is now known as chemical and biomolecular engineering, I chose Lehigh University because I wanted Arthur Humphrey—one of the most respected experts in this field—to be my advisor and also because it was an hour and a half drive to my family's home in Wilmington, Delaware. My father was dying from a rare cancer called malignant fibrous histiocytoma, and I wanted to be near my parents in case they needed me.

I began my graduate student experience with some doubts. As an undergraduate at the College of William and Mary in Virginia, I converted to the Roman Catholic faith to help me make sense of my father's illness and find inner peace. I later witnessed in amazement as both of my parents also converted from our family's United Methodist tradition. That caused me to wonder if my calling was to the church's ministry.

Before I arrived in Bethlehem, I had completed my application to become a Catholic priest in the Diocese of Richmond, Virginia, but set it aside in favor of the "family business" in science and engineering—professions in which both of my parents had achieved success and accolades. On October 27, 1982, my father passed away at the young age of fifty-four. In the years ahead, I would learn to channel my grief and pastoral instincts into leadership skills that put people first.

ORASURE IS FOUNDED

Meanwhile, in December 1987, Mike Gausling and colleagues founded SolarCare Technologies as a startup company spun out of Lehigh University. Their original business plan was to produce and sell sunscreen in single-use wet wipe packs. At that time, I was writing my PhD dissertation. After I completed and defended my thesis and graduated in May 1988, I stayed at Lehigh to become the general manager of its Center for Molecular Bioscience and Biotechnology. In that role, I was a landlord for SolarCare's lab on Lehigh's Mountaintop Campus. This wasn't quite the obscure beginning of a classic Horatio Alger, Jr. "rags-to-riches" story, but it's where my unlikely journey began with OraSure.

Between 1988 and 1992, I was also asked to review and recommend applications from startup life science companies seeking funding from Pennsylvania's Ben Franklin Technology Partners. At the time, Pennsylvania was a pioneer in the use of state money to launch companies and retain jobs. SolarCare later became STC Technologies and then merged with Portland, Oregon-based Epitope Inc. in 2000 to become OraSure Technologies.

I lost touch with the company when I left Lehigh in 1992 to start my career as a general management consultant after earning another degree, this one from The Wharton School of Business's MBA for Executives Program. But I didn't lose touch with CEO Mike Gausling. That's because his son and mine became friends in elementary school. During those years, Mike and I became friendly in the way that parents of children's friends do during our kid's pick-ups and drop-offs and at school and family gatherings.

JOURNEYS IN STRATEGIC LEADERSHIP

I've always been attracted to environments where I can utilize my skills and deliver value in a fast-paced, dynamic way. So, when I had the opportunity to join a general management consultancy that was rapidly growing and working with some of the biggest names in business, I took it. I quickly rose through the ranks at Gemini Consulting, becoming a vice president in only twenty months. I loved putting together project teams and coming up with creative solutions to challenges under tight deadlines.

When strategy consultancy Kearney was acquired by IT service giant Electronic Data Systems Corporation (EDS) in 1996, I saw an opportunity to lead a practice in the life sciences industry and moved on from Gemini after four years. By 1999, I was responsible for managing EDS's account at Johnson & Johnson. This exciting and challenging work allowed me to make a difference for my clients. During my time at J&J I met a key person in my career who I will refer to as "the Client." He hired me to deliver high-impact strategic plans. The Client and I would also be destined to encounter each other again later on in our careers.

The final presentation for that engagement was memorable for the breadth and depth of the analyses and recommendations to J&J's top executives, including the then and future CEO. It was also indelible because I had to have an emergency appendectomy that evening. It would only be far later in my career that I would recognize my drive toward excellence and achievement was so closely linked with my chronically poor health.

In 2000, I took on the role of president and CEO of Millennium Cell, an energy technology startup company. My challenge was to transform a twelve-person laboratory and engineering team into a credible publicly financed company. We went public through an initial public offering (IPO) in August, with only the founder and me on the management team and a barebones business plan. It would be hard to fathom those circumstances happening in today's stock market.

I led the company through IPO and follow-on investment and ensuing strategic, technological, and commercialization challenges. Millennium Cell's market capitalization grew from $8.8 million when I was hired to $300 million at IPO to the peak of $1 billion in November 2000. However, in 2004, the board decided they could run the company differently and better, and I was fired for the first time in my life. By 2008, they were delisted by NASDAQ and went out of business soon after. A certain hollowness in my soul still resonates today because what I had labored long and hard to build wasn't sustained after my painful departure.

Beyond the business experience, the most consequential event during my tenure at Millennium Cell was 9/11. This would be the first of three major crises I would experience as a CEO during my career. The other two were the 2007 recession and the 2020 pandemic. While, today, most people don't list their experiences during major crises, I believe living and learning through those types of events are relevant and will be crucial to the future success of employees and employers.

ORASURE COMES CALLING (PART 1)

Around 2004, Mike Gausling's board of directors at OraSure decided they wanted to change CEOs. Mike and I had gotten to know each other well enough that he urged me to be a candidate to succeed him. He also let me know one of his fellow board members was championing another candidate with a long résumé at J&J. It was the Client.

OraSure hired him as their CEO in 2005. Instead, I became group vice president and general manager of Olympus America's newly combined life science businesses as they moved from Long Island, New York, to the Lehigh Valley. While I would have loved to have been CEO of OraSure in 2005, I took some solace that I was leading Olympus businesses with more than $200 million in revenue, while OraSure was then doing $69 million in revenue.

Also in 2005, I interviewed for the CEO role at the University City Science Center, and was also rejected there. The Science Center is like a university but without faculty and students. Their buildings consist of laboratory-based research, an incubator, an accelerator, and expansion space for startup companies, as well as offices, apartments, and retail establishments for businesses serving their campus and those of the nearby University of Pennsylvania and Drexel University. Strange as it may seem, my appointments with career destiny would eventually land me as CEO at the Science Center in 2008 and then at OraSure in 2018, as far-fetched as that would seem back in 2005.

By the time I received a surprise phone call from the Client-turned-OraSure-CEO in 2011, I would have led during the second major external crisis as a CEO—the Great Recession—this time at the Science Center. Even though the company was not-for-profit, the recession of 2007 to 2009 affected commercial real estate, which was a large portion of their revenue stream, as well as many jobs lost in the broader economy. Because the Science Center's programs to support innovators and entrepreneurs rely on their access to capital to fund their businesses, the sudden and bleak impact of the financial crisis meant they struggled mightily, and the Science Center needed to help them through it. We did so through programs that connected entrepreneurs with talented veterans of the life science industry who were laid off due to the recession, providing financial relief to renters of our offices and laboratories, and other programs. It was innovation applied to crisis to benefit many.

ORASURE COMES CALLING (PART 2)

The surprise 2011 phone call led to a meeting with the Client-turned-OraSure-CEO in his headquarters office on East First Street in Southside Bethlehem, a few blocks away from BethSteel's abandoned blast furnaces and east of New Street (where the crime rate had dropped precipitously since 1982). It was awkward to be in an office that could have been mine in 2005. The Client-turned-OraSure-CEO must have wondered why I stared at his walls and cabinets for so long. In my mind, I was arranging my artwork, diplomas, awards, and tchotchkes in his spaces to picture it as my office. After some cordial small talk about our careers, families, and golf, he shocked me by asking, "Would you like to serve on OraSure's board of directors?" I remember feeling exhilarated by his invitation.

You see, at that time, my then-wife of twenty-five years served me with divorce papers and then moved herself and our three children out of our cavernous marital home. I was barely holding myself together, day by day. I poured myself into my work twenty-four-seven as self-medication for an as yet undiagnosed deep depression. OraSure's CEO's offer, which led to interviews with all other board members and then their approval, helped me feel useful and wanted during a time I was grieving my marriage, missing my children, and unsure of where my life was going.

Once I was voted in by the board, I readily accepted and joined them in May 2011. As I left his office that fateful day of our initial meeting, the Client joked, "And Steve, if I screw up, you can then have my job." Thankfully, he didn't screw up, and I eventually got the job anyway. What was the force behind this improbable twist of fate? Maybe he saw me secretly coveting his office for my own as I arrived, or maybe the universe has an amazing sense of humor about foreshadowing events. In any case, I was about to join a company destined to be an unsung hero in the worlds of genomics, microbiomics, and global public health. I would also learn having and coveting an office wouldn't stand the test of time in 2020.

During my time on the board from 2011 through 2018, Ora-Sure acquired Ottawa, Canada-based DNA Genotek, and launched the world's first FDA-approved home test for HIV. The former was crucial to the company's growth spurt through 2018 because DNA Genotek's saliva home collection kit technology became an indispensable part of 23andMe's and Ancestry's genome kits. The latter was prescient because, until the COVID-19 pandemic, the OraQuick In-Home HIV Test was the only infectious disease home test available in the United States.

During that period, OraSure reached overall profitability but lacked a robust new product pipeline. It was clear we needed to acquire companies and their new products and technologies to continue to grow our revenue. As a small company, this would prove to be challenging without a large amount of cash and corporate development capability that it never had in an organized and sustainable way. These factors became key features of the company's innovation-based growth strategy we unveiled in 2018 under my leadership.

PART 3: THIRD TIME'S THE CHARM

As Jill and I pondered whether I was sure about OraSure in August 2018, my connection and experiences with the company since 1988 all flashed before my eyes. I pictured Solar-Care Technologies' labs on Lehigh's Mountaintop Campus, a chunk of prime real estate that a beleaguered BethSteel sold to the university for one dollar. My career arc from my first apartment in 1982 to OraSure headquarters in 2018, covering a distance of zero point seven miles over thirty-six years, was not exactly warp-speed career velocity, I chuckled to myself. I saw an unhealthy me over those years—from my emergency appendectomy to my depression after divorce, not to mention a lifetime with a high body mass index, a congenitally weakened immune system, a severe bout with Hepatitis B while in graduate school, sleep apnea, and, worst of all, colon cancer.

I saw some unhealthy OraSure board members and senior executives, which led to several early retirements and even a death under mysterious circumstances. During one board meeting, an executive had a cardiac event in the parking lot as he attempted to exit his vehicle. Another time, we were pursuing an acquisition, and our team leader was found unresponsive far from home or workplace with the cause of death indeterminate. We still don't know why this leader was at that location or what happened.

I recalled the strange job interview serendipities in 2005 that would eventually lead to CEO roles at places that originally rejected me—both the Science Center and OraSure. I thought of the commuting irony that had me traveling from home in Lehigh Valley to work in Philadelphia from 2008 to 2013 and the prospect of now traveling from home near Philadelphia to work in the Lehigh Valley. It all seemed a bit surreal.

I knew I would need to make big changes quickly at OraSure to make it a more innovative company. I would also need to break the cycle of poor health for me and OraSure employees by insisting we all take better care of ourselves. Little did I know I'd be facing the third and worst crisis of my CEO career in the COVID-19 pandemic, or that OraSure's genomics business would take a sharp downturn for reasons beyond our control.

From August 2018 to the day I was offered the CEO role in December, I had mixed feelings about taking the job—uncertain whether I was cut out for it. But I knew if I didn't lean in, I would never have the chance to find out what I could do. So, with just enough confidence, I decided to leap forward into the challenge.

As I looked back into the time tunnel of my career, I thought about my lifelong fascination with explorers like Marco Polo and hoped Jill would eventually understand my reasons. I had hopes and dreams of seeking new worlds for innovation throughout my career. Sometimes those hopes and dreams remain long-buried and sprout at unexpected times when given a second or third chance.

Dear Steve...

"As a veteran of OraSure, I have been through five changes to the CEO position. Each one of you has brought different strengths to the organization, and I credit you for our restart of innovation through internal development and external acquisitions, the empowerment of the leadership team to make decisions to help drive the continued success of our organization, and then bringing the organization together during the toughest two years with the COVID-19 pandemic."

CHAPTER 1

The Sound and the Fury

———

"Everyone has a plan until they get punched in the mouth."
—MIKE TYSON, YOUNGEST BOXER EVER
TO WIN A HEAVYWEIGHT TITLE

Few remember it was Evander Holyfield who overcame fifteen-to-two odds against him to defeat Mike Tyson in the epic heavyweight championship boxing match in 1997. Tyson was a brawler, brutal and indomitable at powerfully fighting his way out of a corner and landing devastating blows. How did Holyfield respond to Tyson's unpredictable nature? Could Holyfield have planned to have half of his ear bitten off in this fight? Both Tyson and Holyfield were right in their approaches: Plans don't survive the first punch in the mouth. But you need a plan in the first place to be able to adapt it to changes in reality. Throughout OraSure's history, plans were constantly adjusted for crises, and existential threats were frequently and narrowly avoided.

SIMPLIFYING STRATEGY

Organizations, including OraSure, invest a lot of time and energy into developing strategic plans, which boil down to sets of numbers that forecast profit or loss and project financial statements. These numbers drive expectations both inside and outside the company. I've been involved in this annual process in many organizations as a student, practitioner, advisor, and overseer for most of my career.

For thirty-three combined years of my career, I've held positions as chairman of the board, chief executive officer, or founder/owner. Even when I didn't hold those titles, I developed strategic plans for Fortune 100 companies as a high-powered consultant. So I understand both the value and the drawbacks of having a well-defined strategy. At its best, a strategic plan demonstrates leadership's clarity and honesty about what is known and unknown about the future as well as the organization's commitment to achieving its goals. At its worst, a strategic plan can handcuff an organization because it's viewed as immutable and inflexible.

The strange thing about strategy is we spend so much time and effort on something that, at its core, is relatively simple. Sure, the application of strategy can be complex, but the basic concept is not. Yet we treat it like some holy grail, to be attained only by the elite and learned. This is not to say that strategy is unimportant—far from it. But we should remember that simplicity is often the key to success. After all, $E=mc^2$ is a pretty simple equation, and it describes the entire universe. So, next time you're planning your strategy, keep it simple. It just might be the key to your success.

What's my Occam's razor for strategy? Here's my short and simple description:

The most successful and enduring strategies come from the sweet spot where opportunity and capability overlap.

When we can take advantage of opportunities presented to us, we can create something truly special. But if we're limited in either opportunity or capability, our strategy will suffer. If no good opportunities are available, it won't matter how skilled we are. We won't be able to make anything happen. And if we're not capable of taking advantage of the opportunities that do exist, we'll miss out on valuable chances for success. The key is to find that sweet spot where our skills meet a need in the market and then go for it with everything we've got. That's how the best strategies are born.

We value foresight over hindsight because it allows us to be proactive instead of reactive. By being strategic and anticipating what is to come, we can create plans that increase the chances of success. This not only benefits the organization but also makes us look smarter and more capable. Yet unforeseen elements are bound to complicate our path forward.

CRISES SCUTTLE STRATEGY

A crisis is any situation that throws a wrench in our plans. It might be something small like a client canceling a project or something big like a natural disaster. Whatever the crisis may be, it creates challenges we didn't anticipate and need to address urgently. In times of crisis, it's important to have a clear strategy in place so you can adapt quickly and make the best of the situation. Having a plan gives you a roadmap to follow so you can stay focused on your goals despite unexpected obstacles. Without a strategy, it's easy to get lost and bogged down in day-to-day details, which can lead to even more problems.

If you find yourself amid a crisis, take a step back and assess the situation. What is the new reality you're facing? What do you need to do to adapt? Once you have a clear understanding of the situation, you can develop a plan of action to address it. Remember, crises are often fluid and ever-changing, so it's important to be flexible in your approach and be prepared to adjust your plan as needed. The goal is to get through the predicament as quickly and smoothly as possible so you can get back to business as usual—if you survive it.

When Mike Tyson bit off a chunk of Evander Holyfield's ear during their 1997 rematch, it was the culmination of a long-simmering rivalry. The two had met before in a 1996 bout that ended with Holyfield becoming the first boxer since Muhammad Ali to win the heavyweight title three times. Despite Holyfield's victory, Tyson was heavily favored to win the rematch. That's because Tyson was known as a "crisis fighter" who thrived in the chaos he created. Betting on the crisis fighter seems like a sure thing. But in the end, the man with patience and adjustment prevailed. Holyfield may not have planned to lose part of his ear, but he did benefit from the fact that Tyson's rage ultimately defeated the fury of his chaos. When it comes to crisis leadership, it's often the case that the best strategy is to focus on survival, which allows time and space to later thrive. This was certainly true for Holyfield.

The coronavirus has been a near-perfect opponent for humans, mutating and becoming more insidious over time. Unlike Mike Tyson, it wasn't going to self-annihilate by egregiously self-disqualifying. Throughout the world, strategies to defeat the virus have given way to approaches to cope with it, as global herd immunity seems unattainable. This pandemic has caused devastation on a scale unlike anything we have seen before, and no one was safe from it anywhere.

ORASURE PIVOTS TO COVID-19 TESTING

When the pandemic hit in early 2020, vaccine, drug, testing, and personal protective equipment companies rushed to act as "first responders." OraSure was one of these companies, determined to use our particular expertise and experience to assist in the testing dilemma. Those of us in manufacturing businesses can't claim the bravery of risking physical harm in life-or-death situations like law enforcement officers, paramedics, emergency medical technicians, and firefighters do routinely. Yet our mentality was similar—race into the emergency and get to work using our skills and unique capabilities.

As we announced in our April 6, 2020, press release:

"Lives and global economies are at stake. It's crucial that we understand just how many people are infected with SARS-coronavirus," I shared at that time. "In-home self-testing will dramatically increase the capacity for SARS-coronavirus testing and give our healthcare systems and labs some much-needed breathing room. We believe that the development of an easy-to-use device that delivers accurate results to individuals in their homes can play a significant role in impacting infection rates. We are proud to bring our expertise with quality, rapid, oral fluid self-tests to the battle against the COVID-19 pandemic."

Biomedical Advanced Research and Development Authority (BARDA) Director Rick Bright, PhD, then added, "We need to put tests into people's hands to know their infection status and protect their loved ones. At BARDA, we are continually looking for transformative technologies to combat public health threats, and rapid at-home coronavirus testing would be a game-changer. We know that people can spread COVID-19 without showing any symptoms, and with rapid at-home testing, people could take immediate action to prevent the spread of the virus."

We were counting on our success with OraQuick In-Home HIV Test to help us develop and then clear regulatory standards and manufacture InteliSwab Rapid COVID-19 At Home Test. If we could translate previous product success, our pathway for InteliSwab work would be straightforward and predictable. Spoiler alert: It wasn't. But we didn't know then how large or durable the COVID-19 market would be for our test. The disease was infecting and killing millions of people as we developed our test in early 2020. Yet no one then knew how much worse the pandemic would get nor how much longer it would last.

Nevertheless, we had to try and quantify it so we could justify the cost, time, and effort to pursue the opportunity. During our August 5, 2020, earnings call, I stated, "The Rockefeller Foundation report on testing specifically calls for rapid, convenient tests like the antigen test OraSure is developing to help get the thirty million tests per week, many believe, are needed by November to reduce the spread of COVID-19." That meant there was a larger opportunity here than anything else OraSure had addressed in its twenty years as a public company. Conservative estimates by others projected we could make and sell around one hundred million InteliSwab tests per year for several years.

To put that into perspective, we shared in our November 4, 2020, earnings call that OraSure's "embedded capacity [was] about seventeen million to eighteen million units per year of capacity for our existing HIV, HCV, and Ebola tests." InteliSwab represented a five- to six-fold bigger opportunity for the company's product line. Capitalizing on this opportunity would mean the company needed to completely transform itself while also ensuring everyone was safe and well during a public health crisis. Accomplishing this was a space mission-like moment for us all, and it would mean all of us would be out on a limb to make it happen. It was hard for us and many others to grasp. During 2020 and into 2021, a graph of OraSure's stock price resembled four shark's teeth pointed upward, with sharp rises and falls between $16 and $9 per share, as the stock market struggled to value us and our opportunity.

As we all faced imminent threats to our health, survival, and even existence, I was reminded of a quote from Dr. Mae

Jemison, the first African American female astronaut. She said, "If you think about it, HG Wells wrote *First Men in the Moon* in 1901. Imagine how incredulous, fantastical that idea was in 1901. We didn't have rockets, we didn't have the materials, and we weren't really flying. It was incredible. Less than one hundred years later, we were on the moon" (Weinberger 2014). A COVID-19 rapid home test was fantastical indeed and was a game-changing opportunity for our undersized company.

When I was hired in January 2018, OraSure's board of directors proclaimed in their press release, "We are delighted to welcome Steve as the company's new president and CEO. Steve's vast technical and business experience, both in the private sector and as a public company CEO, and particularly his long and successful track record in developing and commercializing innovative technologies in the life sciences area, make him the ideal executive to lead OraSure into the future."

Since then, I had been focused on executing the company's innovation-based growth strategy and managing the expectations of my board of directors and shareholders. Initially, this plan involved hiring a key executive to help with corporate development and strategy. However, a few months into my tenure, I was informed of the impending retirements of other key leaders. This was not part of the original plan, and it forced me to adapt quickly to manage these crises. Despite these challenges, I remained committed to delivering on the promise of OraSure and renewing our innovation engine.

OPPORTUNITY IN ACQUISITIONS

In a way, a crisis can be also an unforeseen opportunity. Prior to 2018, we didn't foresee we would spend money to pursue and acquire companies. How could we if we couldn't deliver it? Fortunately, my first hire, David Rappaport—now senior vice president of corporate development, strategy, and integration—was supreme at hitting the ground running. He did so while relocating himself and his family from Atlanta, building his team, and earning the respect of his colleagues and the board through detailed analyses, persuasive logic, and his warm and winning grin that he flashed often, even under duress. By the end of 2018, he had landed OraSure's first two acquisitions since 2011: CoreBiome and Novosanis. Both were crucial for our future growth through innovation.

In addition to OraSure's rapid-test products for HIV, Hepatitis C, and Ebola, much of our expected growth was to come from simple ways to sample parts of the body for later analysis in a laboratory, according to the research analysts that covered us. That seemingly trivial contribution is a key to learning more about what's in us, on us, and around us to help people get or stay healthy. It's like photography.

Most of us take for granted that aiming our smartphones at people or places preserves the moment for posterity. Behind the button we push to make it all happen are technologies that ensure we capture and save the moment conveniently and accurately. High-quality optics and software ensure we record the precise moment with all of its color, contrast, and lighting. Storage software uplinked to the cloud ensure the image is maintained for long periods. Later on, anyone with the photo can edit or analyze it with unique data tags carried on every pixel of every image.

Likewise, OraSure's molecular solutions business helps life science researchers take "snapshots" of saliva, urine, feces, and other bodily fluids or surfaces by accurately sampling the mouth, nose, skin, and any orifice. The folks who work in molecular solutions are well aware of the "ick" and "gross" reaction to descriptions of their technology. Because of it, they've normalized bathroom humor into their conversations. "Let's be #1 in the #2 business!" or "Human genomics wouldn't be worth spit without us" are two examples that still make the teenager in me chuckle like Beavis and Butt-Head.

In the wee hours in the waning days of December 2018, David and his colleagues had ample reason to celebrate the addition of Novosanis and CoreBiome into the OraSure family of companies. Novosanis, based in Belgium, brought us a breakthrough urine collection product. Through CoreBiome's capability, we unlocked the stories that DNA and RNA can tell. It's an inside-out and outside-in view of the trillions of bacteria and other microorganisms that make up the microbiome. As scientists and physicians study the effect of the microbiome on digestion, inflammation, mood, neuro-generative disease, and skin disease and appearance, their leading technology will be central to better understanding health and well-being and developing new therapies and cosmetics to improve it.

When he stood in the doorway of my office on December 30, 2018, to let me know that both acquisitions were complete, David flashed his trademark smile with a hint of his doppelganger's intensity—tennis great Novak Djokovic's penetrating stare—and beseeched me with, "Next time, let's try not to close two deals on the same day!"

I replied tongue in cheek, "Okay! Next time, shall we try for three in one day?"

He burst into nervous laughter. Yet we both knew how important this moment was to reset our company's capabilities and culture as part of our innovation-based growth strategy.

MORE ADJUSTMENTS TO STRATEGY

Up to that moment of victory, 2018 had been a tough year for our company. Our biggest customer informed us mid-year that they were drastically reducing their orders. This caused our revenue growth forecasts to be way too high, and our stock price fell from over $21 per share to below $12 per share by the end of 2018.

Customer concentration risk caused this—having too few customers buying most of our products. This surprised the research analysts who covered us. Their financial models predicted we would continue to add sales with this customer over several years. This meant 2019 would be a "down year" for our company revenue compared to 2018. Our plan for 2019 would reflect that foreboding truth yet also plan on the integration of our new acquisitions and the divestiture of a division that wasn't performing to our revenue growth expectations.

We were fortunate to make a third company acquisition in 2019—Diversigen, a premier microbiome services company that had rebuffed our offer in 2018. We quickly planned to merge the operations and staff of CoreBiome and Diversigen into one wholly owned subsidiary. We closed 2019 with new leaders in molecular solutions, operations, and corporate communications. As 2020 began, the stock languished below eight dollars per share, and I was intent on making more leadership changes in the diagnostics business unit and research and development to further bolster our capabilities.

BUILDING ON UNIQUE CAPABILITIES

Without a doubt, OraSure had unique capabilities in the medical diagnostic industry that belied our small size. Until the COVID-19 pandemic, we had the only FDA-approved home test for any infectious disease. The OraQuick In-Home HIV Test hit the market in 2012 heralded by a *New York Times* July 3 front-page story—the upper right column above the fold that proclaimed "Rapid HIV Home Test Wins Federal Approval" (McNeil 2012).

Donald G. McNeil, Jr. wrote, "After decades of controversy, the Food and Drug Administration approved a new HIV test on Tuesday that for the first time makes it possible for Americans to learn in the privacy of their homes whether they are infected. The availability of an HIV test as easy to use as a home-pregnancy kit is yet another step in the normalization of a disease that was once seen as a mark of shame and a death sentence." We believed our in-home HIV test had the potential to be a game-changer for our company.

In 2016, OraQuick In-Home HIV Test also became the only World Health Organization pre-qualified saliva-based HIV test sold outside the United States as a self-test in HIV high-prevalence areas such as sub-Saharan Africa, Asia, and Latin America. By 2018, research analysts who followed us closely knew this global market for our best-selling diagnostic product would begin to wane around 2020 due to the end of our product subsidy agreement with the Bill and Melinda Gates Foundation. We needed strong collaboration between R&D and corporate development to make or buy new products.

DAWN OF THE PANDEMIC

Pursuing collaboration meant many days of travel and discussion across the US and many other countries. I made a trip to Beijing in November of 2019 to immerse myself in the evaluation of a company along with the ceremony of doing business in China. I didn't realize other factors would soon overtake our pursuits.

At that very time, Dr. Xinjing Zhao, a senior executive with a global petroleum company, was in Beijing leading a multibillion-dollar joint venture with the Chinese government. He heard early reports about a flu-like infection in Wuhan and shared his concerns with his superiors in the US. "I guess we were not sure at the beginning what to make of it when it first came out," he said in an interview. "I didn't know then what it meant, but every day it seemed to get scarier."

Dr. Zhao had employees in Wuhan, so his priority was to get them out of the city to a safer location. But his superiors in the US couldn't then grasp the severity or urgency of the early signs of a pandemic. They were eager for routine business progress reports. "People are understandably worried, as they should be, but they are generally not scared," he wrote in his January 30, 2020, LinkedIn newsletter. "Most people do have a relatively high level of trust in the [Chinese] government and believe that the most that could be done is being done" (Zhao 2020).

He continued: "It seems all my family, friends, and colleagues are taking it in their stride. Most streets in Beijing are quiet. While people are bored at home during the extended Chinese New Year holiday, WeChat provides a perfect platform for them to communicate and share information." Many local governments or companies in China were requiring workers or citizens to submit online forms regularly to inform the government of travel and health conditions as preventive measures in case anyone had an infection.

In the coming months and years, I would find myself in the middle of Xinjing's uncertainty and dilemma, witnessing firsthand the wildly different approaches taken by the Chinese and American governments. Virtually every strategy and plan would be derailed by this global health crisis replete with the unforeseen. Could OraSure survive, let alone thrive, under these conditions?

Dear Steve...

"I was terrified when [our company was] acquired [by OraSure]. I had never worked for a public company before but understood enough business to know things would change a lot! I will always remember how you took the time to learn who we were and what our names were, and you always greeted us by name when you saw us. I learned about leadership from watching you, and I know my team did as well."

CHAPTER 2

Mars Mission

———

"We are all in the gutter, but some of us are looking at the stars."
—OSCAR WILDE, IRISH POET, AUTHOR, AND PLAYWRIGHT

When the pandemic first hit, the world was uncertain about what would happen next. Mark Watney, the fictional astronaut from *The Martian*, was faced with a similar uncertainty when he was stranded on Mars. However, unlike Watney, OraSure had to rely on science to deliver us from the potential doom of the virus without anybody coming to our rescue. In other words, we needed to science the shit out of our situation on our own.

Our scientists knew the coronavirus wasn't going to self-destruct and we would need to make products on a scale many times larger than we'd ever experienced. This journey would be inevitably tortuous and stressful but would be worth it in the end because we were able to produce needed tests that saved lives. I had convinced myself of that outcome. Now I just needed to persuade four hundred of my colleagues too.

ORASURE'S SPACE FRONTIER

Space exploration became a compelling and relatable way to share our vision across the company. It appealed to me personally because both my late father and late uncle were recipients of the NASA Lifetime Achievement Award. The award acknowledged my father's innovative work for DuPont on the heat-deflecting tiles that form the skin of the space shuttle. Without the tiles, the shuttle would burn to a crisp on reentry to Earth. My uncle was a chief engineer at NASA's Johnson Space Center and invented the fabric used for space suits that protect astronauts from harm and keep them comfortable.

Through space exploration, we can connect with people on a personal level and inspire them with our vision. It also allows us to honor the innovative work of those who have come before us. As I said in February 2021:

> The year 2021 will be a year of significant change for all of us. It's part of a multi-year transformation that began with our pivot into COVID-19 sample collection and test, last year. We expect our businesses will expand dramatically this year and for the foreseeable future. All of us need to elevate our games.
>
> So, what does "elevate" mean for each of us? The metaphor that I shared at the diagnostics national sales meeting last week was, "We are caterpillars destined to become butterflies on a rocket to Mars."
>
> To me, that means that as we elevate (and slip the bonds of gravity) for this monumental journey to an

unknown world, each of us is challenged to transform to thrive on our way to that destination.

I understand that metamorphosis to a butterfly and a trip to Mars each have excitement and terror built in—which is compounded when both transformations happen simultaneously.

As you unpack what this metaphor means to you and to the OraSure family of companies, please know I understand that change (let alone transformation) is difficult. As the saying goes, "Everyone wants progress, but nobody wants to change." Ultimately, though, as Charles Darwin reminds us, those who thrive are those who best adapt to their environment. I want that for each of us on our journey, because our environment is changing quickly.

Each of us reacts and responds to change differently. Some have an easier time with it than others. If nothing else, 2020 proved that each of us found a way to emerge resilient from the changes to our lives that the pandemic brought about.

I've found that coping with change requires healthy doses of both faith and doubt. I like the way author Sue Monk Kidd describes this tension of opposites in her book, *When the Heart Waits: Spiritual Direction for Life's Sacred Questions*:

"What has happened to our ability to dwell in unknowing, to live inside a question and coexist with the tensions of uncertainty? Where is our willingness to incubate pain and let it birth something new?" she asks. "These things are what form the ground of waiting. And if you look carefully, you'll see that they're also the seedbed of creativity and growth—what allows us to do the daring and to break through to newness... Creativity flourishes not in certainty but in questions. Growth germinates not in tent dwelling but in upheaval" (Monk 1990).

Like creativity, scientific discovery and innovation flourish in questions, and OraSure's growth germinated in the upheaval of the pandemic. As 2021 progresses, we will have growing pains, and we must be willing to deal with them. Yet I assure you the transformations will be well worth it. We have dared, and I have faith that we will break through!

OUR INNOVATION LEADER

The late Steve Jobs said, "Innovation distinguishes between a leader and a follower." In any breakthrough, someone needs to step forward and take a bold yet calculated risk. OraSure's leader for diagnostic research and development was just that person. Dr. Jody Berry is a seasoned immunologist, Canada born and bred, who drove across the US from California in 2018 to join OraSure. Jody arrived shortly after I became CEO.

From the outset, I was impressed by his credentials, calm confidence, and entrepreneurial nature. He could explain science persuasively to those of us making decisions on budgets and staffing. Jody is also a bear of a man—tall, rotund, bigger than life, and still an ice hockey player. I wouldn't want to be checked into the boards by him in hockey *or* immunology. His focus, pride, and modesty percolate through his LinkedIn self-description: "As the creator behind InteliSwab and its inception, I grew accustomed to standing out on a limb as the pandemic accelerated. Since that time, all of OraSure has embraced the device in its execution, regulatory approvals, and sales. A huge team effort and more to come. I would not have got here without the depth of training, key role models, and critical experiences."

We both became grandfathers during the pandemic and talked often about our families. He and I had many pep talks while he was "out on a limb." He was one of many colleagues who battled for results and progress while up against the enormous pressure of time and dealing with personal and family safety, confinement, and isolation. At times, he and I—and many others—were unhinged by the enormity of it all and later regretted our outbursts with quick yet sincere apologies, only to have some of our demons continually reappear as the stress and pressure mounted over two years.

When we think of scientific breakthroughs, we often imagine Archimedes-type moments—sudden flashes of insight that lead to major discoveries. In reality, most breakthroughs are the result of years of hard work, monetary investment, and trial and error—with many, many errors. We all experienced this firsthand during the COVID-19 pandemic when we saw how long it took to develop vaccines, drugs, tests, and personal protective equipment. Each had its own challenges. We were reminded that true innovation takes time—even in the face of a global emergency. If we want to be prepared for the next pandemic, we need to invest in the slow, steady work of scientific research for the long term.

Top research and development teams regularly scan scientific journals for new information that could help with existing products or inspire ideas for new ones. When many of them read early accounts of the virology of COVID-19 in 2020, they were convinced this infection would be much worse than the SARS outbreak of 2002 to 2004.

Because the company—and the R&D team, in particular—had a close working relationship with the Biomedical Advanced Research and Development Authority (BARDA)—a key US government funding agency and thought leader—we met with them with all due haste. BARDA leadership was highly receptive to a funding proposal from OraSure to develop this test. Within sixty days, we were awarded funding and began development—except for two problems.

Like many people in early 2020, the laboratory staff at R&D were reluctant to return to the lab and resume work for fear of their health and safety. Jody and his team provided protocols for masking, gloving, and distancing within the labs that were supported by outside data on protection from infection. This was my earliest pandemic lesson on what is personal is universal. By convincing the scientists they would be safe from viral transmission in our labs, we convinced them to get back to work developing a test to help the world stay safe from the virus. That virtuous symmetry was crucial and essential to our success and trust in each other.

Eventually, the R&D laboratory staff returned to the labs, and our pursuit of InteliSwab was underway in April 2020. Soon after, Jody informed me he wanted to shuffle some roles on his team and bring in three new senior leaders. At first, this seemed like a crazy request. We had a hard enough time convincing scientists in Bethlehem to return to the labs that were a few miles away from the safety of their homes. Now, he thought we could relocate people from California and Florida to humble "Christmas City USA"—Bethlehem's moniker—during a pandemic? As it turns out, he could and did. Soon enough, a cadre of scientific experts would arrive, from near and far, with leadership critical to our success.

"EMBRACE THE SUCK"

In a crisis, it's important to "embrace the suck" and accept it at any given moment, according to Shawn Engbrecht, author of *Invisible Leadership* (Engbrecht 2018). Embracing the suck means accepting reality and not sugarcoating the situation. This is important because if everyone on staff realizes there is a problem, they won't be reassured by an executive blithely promising it may go away. Acceptance of reality is key in a crisis.

A good leader must take time to listen to staff concerns and answer their questions. That may require a bit of patience. As R&D was heads-down developing InteliSwab, the rest of us looked at every aspect of what would be needed to become a company that had a significant positive effect on the pandemic. No stone was left unturned, from new buildings and manufacturing lines to laboratories and air purification systems. It's every CEO's job to decide on priorities and timing for these projects and their costs, seek and land strategic partnerships, and obtain approval from the board of directors. In the end, we presented a convincing case and were off and running. Part of our case was to demolish the corporate offices—including my own—to build the new manufacturing lines. The next step was to overcome inevitable inertia.

The Lego Movie is a 3-D computer-animated family adventure from 2014 that tells the story of Emmet, an average member of the ultra-peppy Lego society (Lord and Miller 2014). Emmet is anointed by an underground resistance movement as the "Special"—the one person who can save the world from the secret scheming of its nefarious leader, President Business. His evil master plan is to make the status quo a permanent reality by supergluing everyone in place—into permanent inertia.

Emmet, meanwhile, must learn to stop slavishly following "the instructions," improvise, and think the unthinkable. The crux of the drama is not whether the world will be saved or destroyed. It's whether "Don't change anything" will triumph over "You can still change everything." The Lego people had to come to grips with the shift from staking everything on the preservation of the familiar to embracing the unknown.

CATALYST FOR POSITIVE CHANGE

While OraSure didn't face the "either-or" drama of Legoland, there was bound to be tension between old ways and new ways of doing our work. When Lisa Nibauer came on board as the leader of the diagnostics business unit in 2020, she catalyzed a company-wide sense of urgency and brought a wealth of experience that set her apart from her colleagues. With an intensely analytical mind, penetrating blue eyes, and a friendly, positive yet no-nonsense attitude, Lisa quickly made a name for herself as a hard-working agent for change.

Though her direct approach may have triggered an immune response from some at first, her colleagues soon came to respect her for her expertise, unrivaled work ethic, and dedication to progress. My job was to balance the tension and harmony needed for us all to advance as far as possible toward results with speed but not haste. Thanks to Lisa's fresh perspective and sheer will, we made incredible progress in a short amount of time.

When results from R&D showed the mouth wasn't the best place to sample the coronavirus, we had to modify the design of the swab portion of InteliSwab to sample from the nose. This came during a skittish time for our stock price, which fell from $16.50 per share on July 20, 2020, to $10.24 per share at the end of August. Some investors thought we had missed our window of opportunity because the pandemic would soon be over. Others thought our behemoth competitors—Abbott and Quidel—were unbeatable in the marketplace. Obviously, we still needed to win over the hearts and minds of many people to make InteliSwab a success.

Meanwhile, Lisa moved quickly to hire capable leaders who brought new perspectives to marketing and clinical operations. As product development adjusted to the new design, we entered the phase of optimizing performance by minimizing false positives (that is, uninfected people who test positive) and false negatives (infected people who test negative). Figuring that out was a deceptively fraught process that required thousands of precisely designed experiments and process iterations under duress and tight deadlines.

CHALLENGES ABOUND

Before the pandemic, medical diagnostic companies generally relied on a large body of science previously validated with well-established specifications from the FDA to drive product development and clinical trials. However, in 2020, the world was just learning about the virology and immunology of the coronavirus, and we were all adapting to it as quickly as possible. In my overall career experience, the inevitable dead ends, rework, and recycling of effort took a toll on research and development teams because they made up for those inefficiencies by working harder and longer hours under the best of circumstances. I wanted to ensure we were sensitive to signs of burnout and elevated it along with employee safety and well-being on the list of compassionate priorities to support our people. Nevertheless, we saw signs of burnout often and had to frequently cope with them.

As companies raced to develop and get FDA clearance for COVID-19 rapid tests, the demand for service firms that design and manage clinical trials was never higher. Across the industry, scheduling these trials was difficult in the best of times, but around the end-of-year holidays, it became a nightmare for many companies. As crazy as it sounds, I heard often of companies adjusting their decisions and actions to sync with a maddening twenty-four-hour news cycle covering the virus. As an industry, we were navigating uncharted seas in harsh weather.

RETHINKING CONFLICT

As 2021 began, vaccines became available, and our company's transformational efforts lurched forward. I revisited the Mars imagery and coupled it with recent work from Adam Grant. Grant's book, *Think Again*, argues that it is important to have people around us who will challenge our ideas and help us see our blind spots, which is especially important for leaders, who should listen to criticism more often and use it to make us stronger. In polite company, it is easy to shy away from conflict, but Grant believes constructive conflict can be helpful. It allows us to explore different perspectives and learn from one another. I shared:

> It's important to remember that not all conflict is personal. "The notion of a spirited debate captures something important about how and why good fights happen," Grant explains. "In good fights, the tension is intellectual, not emotional. The tone is vigorous and feisty rather than combative or aggressive. They don't disagree just for the sake of it; they disagree because they care" (Grant 2021, 88).

> It may seem counterintuitive, but I believe this type of constructive challenge has a place in our culture. It can help us embrace a different perspective on teamwork and impact our future success.

In closing, this has been a particularly challenging week for our colleagues in Houston. Most, if not all of them, are experiencing the negative impact of the recent storms and sub-freezing temperatures—with no heat, hot water, or electricity, burst pipes, and treacherous road conditions. It's made me realize how many of life's basic comforts we take for granted—and how distressing and scary it can be when they are disrupted. My heart goes out to the Houston team. We're ready to help in any way we can.

COPING WITH NATURAL DISASTER

Even as I tried to focus our Herculean effort on our "Mars Mission" goal and speak to the inevitable tension and friction between people during our pursuit, we had to also cope with historically severe weather conditions that threatened a key company location. In February 2021, Winter Storm Uri hit Texas and crippled the state as temperatures dropped to as low as six degrees. Extreme weather conditions and winter power grid failures made living conditions unbearable for our Diversigen team in Houston. That prompted this reply from an R&D director:

Thanks for including a message about last week's winter storm in Texas. It was a new experience for me, having grown up in Pennsylvania and dealt with my share of cold weather and winter storms. But the combination of the storm with power, water, and communication disruptions amid a pandemic was tough.

I'm so glad that power was restored on Wednesday morning and that we were able to find some groceries yesterday after an apocalyptic trip to the store on Friday. Finally receiving an "all clear" notice about our boil water advisory was a huge relief. It's easy to take life's basic comforts for granted until they're suddenly gone.

I think it's safe to say that we Houstonians know to prepare for hurricane season (which is June through November), but we let our guard down a bit when it comes to winter. Lessons learned.

I thought of the apocryphal words of Saint Teresa of Calcutta: "I know God will not give me anything I can't handle. I just wish that He didn't trust me so much." What else could happen next?

BREAKTHROUGH TO FDA CLEARANCE

By the spring of 2021, we submitted InteliSwab to the FDA for emergency use authorization (EUA). That set off two months of intensive discussion with the agency, as they were defining performance and use criteria for COVID-19 self-tests. Close collaboration during this time was crucial because our submission came before their definition of requirements.

Finally, on June 4—Lisa Nibauer's birthday—we received EUAs for InteliSwab and could begin selling our product. The focus then turned to manufacturing to make as many tests as possible as soon as possible and to sales and marketing to sell and manage customer expectations. Those would prove to have enormous challenges.

But for now, it was time to celebrate as I remarked then:

> As a company, OraSure is *The Little Engine That Could.* We have all climbed some steep mountains this year— professionally and personally, and I strongly believe our greatest days are ahead of us! "I know we can!" Just as the book says…

InteliSwab would eventually be named the "easiest to use" COVID-19 self-test by Oprah Winfrey's publication, awarded government purchasing contracts for hundreds of millions of dollars, be further cleared by FDA for use by children ages two and older, win the Platinum Award for Infectious Disease Control from *Occupational Health & Safety* magazine, and be named the "#1 standout product" to hit drugstore shelves in 2021 by Drug Store News. It's been used by entertainers from Sheryl Crow to the Counting Crows and many others to ensure that their touring companies are healthy and safe.

Against all odds, the tiny company in Bethlehem, Pennsylvania, was more than surviving. We were on our way to thriving.

Dear Steve...

"I have learned a ton of valuable lessons from you on how to lead an organization during a very difficult time with COVID-19. I still remember our first one-on-one meeting. We got to the end of the meeting when I had exhausted my questions. You had a million things to do and could easily have ended the call five minutes early, but instead you took the time to ask two things: How was I doing, and how was my team doing? It seems minor, but it meant a lot."

CHAPTER 3

Beyond Survival

———

"To us, health is about so much more than simply not being sick. It's about getting a balance between physical, mental, emotional, cultural, and spiritual health. Health and healing are interwoven, which means that one can't be separated from the other."

—DR. TAMARA MACLEAN, AUSTRALIA'S FIRST
FEMALE ABORIGINAL PHYSICIAN

On Mars, fictional astronaut Mark Watney in *The Martian* is injured and left for dead. He soon realizes his only chance for survival is to come to grips with his harsh environment and dismal circumstances. As he struggles to adapt and fight back against isolation and loneliness, he becomes increasingly desperate. In *The Martian*, we witness the powerful effects isolation can have on even the strongest minds. Through Watney's story, we learn it is possible to overcome great adversity if we are willing to fight for our survival.

When we closed the OraSure offices on Friday, March 13, 2020, we sent most of our employees around the world into their own form of isolation. Lots of other companies and people faced the same dilemma. For many of us, this was the first time to experience anything like this. We suddenly had to find ways to work and live without much in-person interaction. For some, this was a welcome change. They found they could be more productive without the distractions of colleagues. Some missed the interaction and connection with others. Some struggled with the lack of structure and routine.

No matter how people felt about it, isolation was a new challenge for all of us. We had to find ways to stay connected and support each other through this time. It's been years since the pandemic started, and we are still living with its effects. During this time, we have learned a lot about ourselves and each other. We have also learned how to be more flexible and adaptable. This experience has changed us in many ways, and we ought to be grateful for the lessons we have learned.

IT'S ABOUT TRUST, SIMPLY DEFINED

Before we could be a latter-day HG Wells and envision space travel before it was imaginable, we needed to make sure we could trust each other, which meant cultivating trust between us and making sure everyone was alive, sentient, and functional. Back when I was a management consultant with Gemini Consulting, we had a trust formula:

Trust = (Credibility x Intimacy)/Risk

High credibility means you believe someone because there's no gap between what they say and do. You know you can rely on them. High intimacy means you feel safe discussing something with them because you know they have your back. When the stakes are high, the risk is high. So, when there's perceived danger, credibility and intimacy need to soar to meet the challenge. The company's survival—not to mention its transformation—depended on constantly and vigilantly building trust, as individuals and as teams. But first, we all needed to survive.

Nearly three months after our offices closed, we established clear guidelines for our survival.

> The OraSure family of companies is committed to keeping our employees safe and healthy. We know the current crisis is caused by a new virus for which there is no treatment or vaccine. This means that people can easily spread the virus to others, especially in places where they work. Until we find a way to stop the virus from spreading, we will do everything we can to keep our employees safe.
>
> We don't have all the information we need about the virus yet. This means it's hard to know who has the virus (and can spread it), who has had it before (and might not get it again), and who has never had it (and could get it). If we knew these things, it would be easier to manage the crisis.
>
> Our only solution right now is to help our people interact less, physically. This could mean changing

the way our workspaces are designed (to have fewer chances for people to interact or touch things), how we do workflows (doing them one person at a time instead of together), and how we manage people (so there are fewer interactions between different groups or teams). We are thinking about all of these options. Until we are sure that we need to change our "work from home if you're able to do so" policy, we will stay in our current mode.

FALSE START TO A NORMAL SUMMER

Of course, those companies in June 2020 who were making back-to-office plans would soon have their hopes dashed by the rise of the more virulent Delta and then Omicron variants. For the OraSure employees who weren't able to work from home, we acknowledged their plight and the risks they took to do their important jobs for us. They endured the hardships of gowning, masking, and gloving for eight to sixteen hours a day, taking breaks, or eating lunch in small groups apart from each other, sometimes in the cold outdoors of winter while we expanded our facilities. We tried to ease their mind and burdens about infecting their homes and families by rigorously enforcing these safety protocols. We also made it worth their while by increasing their compensation at times for exceptional work under difficult conditions.

Just two weeks later, as people were anxious to enjoy summer in some way, I commented:

As we move into summer, it looks like we're heading back to pre-pandemic life. States are loosening restrictions, schools and universities are sharing their plans for the fall semester, and some professional sports have announced their return.

But there may be some bumps along the way. In the US, for example, optimism about reopening has been tempered by news of spikes in COVID-19 in some states. Planning for a second wave seems to be focused on when, not if.

We must proceed with caution and stay safe and healthy. I encourage everyone to take care of themselves—physically, mentally, emotionally, and spiritually. I know how hard everyone is working as we maximize our business opportunities and do things the right way. Even so, in these stressful times, it's more important than ever to maintain a work-life balance. While abiding by safety and health precautions, please be sure to dedicate time to your family, loved ones, friends, and to yourself. This is especially important for those who live and work in communities that are experiencing grief, unrest, and uncertainty.

Above all, remember that OraSure is here to help. Please reach out if you need anything.

As Dr. Oliver Wendell Holmes, Sr., the physician, poet, and father of a Supreme Court Justice, once said: "To reach a port we must sail, sometimes with the wind, and sometimes against it. But we must not drift or lie at anchor." In other words, we can't get stuck in bad places as a company or as individuals.

COVID-19, a renewed social consciousness, and other forces continue to change the direction of the winds, and we continue to adjust our sails. I am confident that together we will reach our destination. I, for one, am glad we're on this journey together.

In June 2020, the American death toll due to COVID-19 had risen to one hundred ten thousand with a base rate of ten thousand dead per week. The top official in Washington stated that the virus was fading away and suggested slowing down testing because it would only result in detecting more cases. These statements and many others have been perceived by many as inaccurate, deceptive, or both at different points throughout the pandemic.

"Stay safe. Be well" became my mantra to assure employees that their well-being was our primary goal, even when some government leaders sounded like they were offering denials and misdirection. Unlike the echo chambers of social media and broadcast news, I never referenced any world leader making statements I knew to be wrong, so as not to add to the ever-present cacophony and confusion. As the old saying goes, trouble arises not from lack of knowledge but from believing false things to be true. Equally important was that we acknowledged what we didn't know and focused on the important questions that needed to be answered.

Recall that back in the summer of 2020, we didn't know the importance vaccines would have in living with the coronavirus and preventing deaths and severe illnesses because we didn't yet know vaccines could be developed and deployed so quickly. It seems obvious now, but there was much then we didn't know. Trust was built by acknowledging the unknown and siding with caution and safety. Trust had to be unassailable to endure the many waves of new infections and complications yet to come. Through diligence and good fortune, OraSure had few cases of COVID-19 among our global workforce in 2020 and 2021.

FOCUS ON HEALTH

We needed to move beyond safety precautions and become healthier people for the sake of our collective mission and transformation. As individuals, we have lives beyond our livelihoods, and we need to be healthy to live them fully. By becoming healthier people, we could make a stronger positive impact on the world around us.

I opined in the late summer of 2020:

> It's been twenty weeks since we've been in quarantine, and I'm grateful for all the hard work everyone has put in. These have been trying times, but our team has risen to the challenge. I want to especially thank those of you who are working in our manufacturing, maintenance, quality control, warehouse, and research and development facilities. It's not easy to work under these conditions, yet you are doing an amazing job. I also want to thank those of you who are working from home. It's not always easy to be

productive when there are so many interruptions and distractions, yet you are doing a great job, too.

As we enter the dog days of summer, we must stay energized. This is going to be a busy time as our businesses ramp up, thanks to our COVID-19-related products and several of our core businesses. I know there is still a lot of uncertainty about how we are going to conquer COVID-19, but we will get through this. In the meantime, we must take care of ourselves. We need to listen to our bodies and make sure we are taking care of our minds and souls.

This has been a learning experience for me. Over the past month, I've had to adjust my running routine due to some minor, but nagging, injuries to my legs. Alternating biking days and running days is helping me rehab my legs. I've also sought care through integrative medicine. This week, I'm almost back to "normal."

It's been a lesson of both frustration and patience—adjusting and readjusting healthy routines. I encourage you to make the adjustments you need in your life to deal with injury, stress, or inconvenience. I hope you'll find ways in your everyday routine, vacation days, and self-care to strengthen yourselves.

Recreation and vacation both involve taking a break from regular life. When you recreate, it's important to remember the meaning of the word: to create something anew. Similarly, the root of vacation is "vacate," or to leave your normal habits for some time. Taking some time away from your daily routine can help you to better appreciate the world around you and come back refreshed. Enjoy your break!

We offered video-conference versions of yoga, stress relief, and meditation to connect physical health to mental, emotional, and spiritual health throughout the pandemic. By doing so, we hoped to help people healthily manage their stress and anxiety.

In April 2021, I spoke of reengaging with other humans to help their well-being.

If you're struggling with the fallout from a year of social isolation, you're not alone. Behavioral health providers are seeing an increase in patients dealing with anxiety, depression, and other issues. Here are some tips for healthily reconnecting with others.

Family struggles, health issues caused by chronic stress, kids with learning or behavioral problems, substance abuse, and loneliness are all part of what we now have to address. If you or your loved ones need help, I urge you to seek it.

We all may need some practice at reconnecting with others—when the time is right and the restrictions in place in our local communities allow. The next time you go to the grocery store or pick up a to-go order, make it a point to have a short conversation with the cashier.

Look that person in the eye. Smile with your lips and eyes under your mask. Ask how their day is going. Or make some sort of comment about how your day is going. As a natural introvert, it's often difficult for me to make small talk. Yet, I know it's worth the effort because I now understand the benefits to me and the other person.

Of course, it's also important to consider your health and the well-being of those around you as you begin to interact with others more. Follow guidelines from local authorities and the CDC to stay safe and healthy. With a little effort, we can all begin to rebuild our social connections healthily.

PERSONAL TRAGEDY

Despite my best efforts to ensure the health and well-being of those I loved and cared for at work, I couldn't avoid a personal health tragedy close to home. At the end of 2020, I nearly lost my wife. It was Christmas Day, and we had decided to venture out of our home and visit some friends nearby. We were part of a small group of people who limited our non-distanced social interaction to each other—a pandemic pod.

As Jill went to hang up our coats in what looked like a small closet, she fell to the bottom of the basement steps. The closet was the top landing for the basement staircase, which neither Jill nor I knew about. I'm grateful she didn't fall on her head, which could have killed her. As it was, she broke her ribs and shoulder while injuring her back severely. The image of her tiny body crumpled at the bottom of a dark basement still haunts me and sends adrenaline coursing through my veins.

I gingerly helped Jill up the stairs and into our car and drove her to a hospital nearby our home. I waited in the parking lot while she was inside the hospital emergency room, weeping, feeling helpless, afraid, and still shocked. Jill sent me text updates over the next six hours before they released her with what little energy she could muster beyond coping with her severe pain.

The pandemic has changed my life in many ways, but most importantly, it has taught me to appreciate and show deep compassion for frontline healthcare workers and those patients who have been separated from their loved ones when they are needed the most. As the leader of OraSure, it became my cause to foster an environment where everyone was appreciated and embraced as whole people—not just employees—with all the challenges of health, safety, and well-being that goes into being fully human. I believe when we practice this kind of openness, acceptance, and support, we can truly make a difference in the lives of those around us.

LET'S TALK ABOUT FAITH

Very few CEOs would dare discuss religion or spirituality with their employees. It's such a personal topic and treads too closely to US Equal Employment Opportunity Commission (EEOC) requirements for workplaces to be free of religious discrimination. But then the pandemic hit, and confinement within our homes and restrictions about gathering cut many of us off from our houses of worship. Over time, some pastors resorted to video-conferencing to share worship, but even so, our worship rituals were disrupted, and our connection to our faith communities was tenuous.

But now, as we start to emerge from this pandemic, perhaps it's time for CEOs to reconsider talking about religion at work. Yes, it's a sensitive topic but one that can provide solace and comfort to employees during these trying times. After all, if we can't turn to our workplaces—where we devote so much of our lives—for support and understanding during a generational crisis, we aren't bringing our whole selves to work.

In September 2020, I shared part of my faith journey.

> When it comes to religious traditions, my family runs the gamut—Protestant, Catholic, Buddhist, and Jewish. I got a crash course in Judaism when I married my wife, Jill, three years ago. Now, I get to celebrate a New Year three times over—on January 1, Chinese New Year, and Rosh Hashanah. Reflecting on all of this has me thinking about what religions teach us, universally. Growing up, I was raised Methodist. But in college, I felt a different spiritual calling and converted to Catholicism. Soon after that, my parents converted too. My mother is now one of the most active members of her parish.
>
> I have immense respect for those who are devout in their religious beliefs and who lead with love, unity, and inclusion. That said, I'm not currently drawn to

organized religion. I remain open to future possibilities, though. For now, as a scientist, I find cognitive and spiritual space between science and religion helps me interpret my world. No matter what your religious beliefs (or lack thereof) are, I hope you're open to your spiritual journey and making peace with your beliefs. And in case you're wondering—according to a recent Pew Research Center survey—atheists and agnostics know more about religion than most other religious groups!

As we head into Rosh Hashanah, I wish everyone a L'shanah tovah—the Hebrew blessing for a good and sweet year. I think we especially need it this year! May you be blessed and be a blessing to others.

I was pleasantly surprised when some of my colleagues shared their own deeply personal stories about their religious or spiritual heritage. It showed me that connection is more important than the risk of violating EEOC guidelines, which we didn't. When it became clear that the "Hot Vax Summer" wasn't going to happen due to the Omicron variant, I looked to the cosmos for inspiration.

Recently, I found myself thinking about a quote from Dr. Albert Einstein: "There are only two ways to live your life. One is as though nothing is a miracle. The other is as though everything is a miracle." It's easy to see why being thankful is a healthy practice. But I would go further and say that everything in life is a miracle.

Think about it. Before the Big Bang happened, there was creativity, energy, and power that was so great it produced light, gravity, time, and space. Galaxies, stars, planets, and oceans were created out of this huge explosion of goodness. And we are just one tiny part of this vast universe. When I look at all that has happened in the world this year, it can be easy to get caught up in the negative. But if I take a step back, I can see there is so much to be thankful for.

Even during a pandemic, we have been able to accomplish amazing things. We have found new ways to connect. We have been more creative in our work. We have been more present with our families. We have learned to support each other. We have been resilient and persevered. It's important to remember that even though the world might seem like a dark place sometimes, there is still so much good in it. And we are all a part of that goodness. So, let's remember to be thankful for everything—the big things and the small things. Everything is a miracle.

Most real-life astronauts who have spent time in space come back to Earth with a renewed appreciation for our planet and its people. For Anousheh Ansari, an Iranian American engineer and the first woman space tourist, the view of Earth from space was emotional. "I felt the warmth and energy and life sort of coming from this incredible planet in front of me, which was my home," she said. "Somehow I was outside of it and very connected to it" (McCann 2021).

Viewing Earth in its entirety from afar gives many astronauts more respect for the planet. "I never was a big crunchy tree hugger kind of person," First Engineer Chris Cassidy said. "But when you've seen the planet from that viewpoint, it makes you appreciate the planet. The atmosphere is so thin, and you realize that that's what keeps all seven billion of us alive. Earth is a spaceship for all of us" (McCann 2021).

In some metaphoric and cosmic way, it was my calling and vocation to bring people together and work in a common cause for our planet, even as we all were isolated and at times lonely, burned out, and fed up with our world. What enabled us to rise to the challenge and thrive?

I believe our shared sense of purpose helped us overcome these challenges. We all knew what we were doing was important, not just for ourselves but for the health and future of humanity. And that knowledge gave us the strength to keep going when things got tough. So, if you're ever feeling lost or alone, remember that you are part of something much bigger than yourself. And that shared sense of purpose will help you overcome any crisis or obstacle.

Dear Steve...

"The 'mind, body, spirit' approach that you have infused into our culture during this pandemic has been refreshing and appreciated."

CHAPTER 4

Flourishing

———

"At the heart of leadership is the leader's relationship with followers. People will entrust their hopes and dreams to another person only if they think the other is a reliable vessel."
—DAVID GERGEN, AUTHOR OF EYEWITNESS TO POWER

In her July 22, 2022, episode of *Firing Line with Margaret Hoover* on PBS, the host opens her show by discussing renowned author and work-life guru Adam Grant's most-read article on the *New York Times* website from 2021 (Hoover 2022), "There's a Name for the Blah You're Feeling: It's Called Languishing." Grant argued that Americans were collectively feeling a sense of languishing. By naming the feeling, we can begin addressing the pervasive stagnation and emptiness. With the coronavirus persisting and lingering concerns about the economy, war, and political polarization, Grant believes a lot of people are still languishing because of these circumstances.

"Languishing is the neglected middle child of mental health. Unlike depression, you still have hope. And unlike burnout, you still have energy," says Grant. But you feel a little bit aimless and a little bit joyless. It's a real thing, and none of us were immune to it during the height of the pandemic. He asserts there's something we can do about it to move toward flourishing, which is the peak of well-being. Flourishing is when you feel like you have a sense of mastery, you have meaning, and you matter to other people. So how do people move from languishing to flourishing?

When Scott Kelly lived on the International Space Station for a year, he had to prepare himself mentally for the challenges of living off the planet. He did this by imagining the future and looking forward to the small wins every day. It's important to have something to look forward to in tough times, and Kelly says imagining the future can help with this.

Having a sense of progress is key to avoiding stagnation, and Kelly believes celebrating small wins every day is a great way to create that sense of progress. The best thing about progress is it's the number one predictor of daily joy and energy at work—just feeling like you're moving forward on a goal. I think that's so important because if stagnation is languishing, then progress is the opposite of stagnation.

To escape languishing, it is important to look to the past for lessons on resilience and have an exciting vision of the future to provide hope. By examining what has kept us motivated and enthusiastic in difficult times before, we can learn a great deal about how to overcome adversity. Our past experiences can teach us a lot about how to cope with stress and setbacks, and having a positive outlook on the future can give us the motivation we need to keep going.

OraSure's success during the pandemic can be attributed to our focus on the present and our ability to "mental time travel" to the past and future. We knew InteliSwab would enable a future free of confinement, and this motivated us to master the work of the present. This symmetry was perhaps subconscious, but it was based on our company's past experiences with OraQuick rapid tests for HIV and Hepatitis C. Our pre-pandemic motto was "Knowledge is power, and testing is the first step toward treatment and care." For InteliSwab and the future, all we needed to add was "and return to a life we once knew."

So, what enabled this to happen? The key was leadership based on compassion, empowerment, accountability, and engagement. In his 2022 update to his seminal book on leadership, *In Discover Your True North*, Bill George, acclaimed former Medtronic Chairman and CEO, and his co-author Zach Clayton profiled behaviors for leaders to enable compassion, empowerment, accountability, and engagement as follows (George and Clayton 2022). I've added "interpret" to number three.

1. Align around the mission.
2. Treat others as equals.
3. Listen, learn, interpret, and share.

ALIGNED AROUND MISSION

The most empowering condition of all is when the entire organization aligns with its mission, and people's passions and purposes synchronize with each other. Getting to this position is not easy, especially if the work environment and the skills and experiences needed are rapidly changing. Nonetheless, it is worth whatever effort it takes to create an aligned environment.

This includes hiring new people into key positions who have traveled further down the road than we have on a common journey, respect for those who established our current ways of doing things while knowing we need to change our ways for the future, and removal of those who don't support the mission. By taking these steps, we can create an organization that is truly empowering for everyone.

When OraSure set out to define its pandemic mission, all of us knew the company's product would play a crucial role in getting the world back to some semblance of normal. Beyond that, OraSure faced the challenge of seeing itself and its emerging needs for talent and experience in objective yet human terms. New and necessary ways of doing things had to be accepted and assimilated by large numbers of people who were used to doing things the old way.

Very few people were exempt from sudden and lasting change. The company needed to help those who were used to a slower or less complex pace of work change their mindset, outlook, and way of doing their jobs. Only then could OraSure hope to achieve its mission.

In a world that is constantly changing, leaders need to embrace and cultivate the tension that comes with it. As the old saying that's attributed to many goes, "Everyone wants progress, but nobody wants change." By having difficult conversations and calling out barriers to change, we can create progress. These conversations could often be deeply emotional experiences, with clashes of personalities and communication styles on full display. However, they were necessary to move us forward.

As a leader, I came to understand our struggles weren't an anomaly. The whole world was being tested in a similar manner. Drawing upon this insight, I helped propel my team forward despite any roadblocks we encountered. Yet what I didn't realize until later on was the critical significance of board members being in alignment with one another when dealing with external pressures. This issue became a portent of danger for me as I worked tirelessly to bring everyone together to reach our lofty goals.

TREAT OTHERS AS EQUALS

Leaders need to respect people who treat them as equals and rely on relationships for their source of power rather than hierarchy. According to research, companies and managers must shift their thinking when it comes to how power is distributed within the organization to succeed in increasingly remote and hybrid work settings. General Stanley McChrystal led the Joint Special Operations Command (JSOC) using a model of "radical transparency," which democratized information sharing by quickly disseminating information not just up the chain of command but across it (Meyer 2020). By empowering those forces to make decisions on their own, they gain momentum and build their leadership skills.

Organizations that rely on hierarchy for their source of power rather than relationships tend to make slower and lower-quality decisions. Relational power enables mixed-level meetings where people with vital contributions to projects or discussions are at the table or video screen because their contribution is valued, not because of their title or reporting relationship.

Relational power is also vital to enable empowerment and accountability together, especially if high-quality and high-velocity decisions are vital to progress. With radical transparency, information is quickly disseminated not just up the chain of command but across it, so everyone has a "shared consciousness" of what is going on. For OraSure, this allowed decision-making authority to be pushed down to lower levels, where people who were well-informed and close to the problem could make decisions to solve it.

McChrystal calls this model "empowered execution" (Meyer 2020). Battles are not won by generals, he says, but by privates and sergeants on the frontlines. If decision-makers have to wait for information to travel up the chain of command, by the time it reaches the frontline force again, the decision could be wrong, outdated, or ill-informed. By empowering those forces to make decisions on their own, they gain momentum and build their leadership skills.

The value of having a clear and concise mission cannot be overstated—something OraSure understood well in our response to the pandemic. Having employees who are focused on the mission at hand is crucial for any organization, but it is especially important in times of crisis. As General McCrystal says, "That's where the rubber meets the road, and that's where they need to be most reactive, most adaptable, most focused on the mission at hand" (Meyer 2000). Leaders need to be present and available to their teams to make this happen.

In that sense, a leader's role is more like a gardener than an order-barker. "When we think about leaders creating an organization, what they're doing is creating an environment or an ecosystem in which the people in the organization—the junior leaders and even the most junior people—can do that which only they can actually do, which accomplishes the mission," says McChrystal (Meyer 2000).

This analogy of leaders as gardeners cultivating future leaders who then help create success highlights how important it is for organizations to treat each other as equals and hold everyone accountable to achieve more than they could have imagined. By doing the right things for the right reasons with passion and engagement, organizations can create ecosystems as lush as rainforests ripe with ingenuity.

LISTEN, LEARN, INTERPRET, AND SHARE

The ability to listen actively is one of the most important skills for empowering leaders. When people feel heard, they sense the leader is assuredly interested in them and not just trying to get something from them. Active listening also shows respect and humility, two essential qualities for effective leadership. As Bill George shared in his book, the best advice he ever got about teaching came from a colleague who warned him not to enter a classroom unless he intends to gain knowledge from the students within.

This advice has informed George's approach to teaching MBA students and executives for the past several years. He tells his students he's confident he'll gain more from his interaction with them than they will from him. The students find this hard to believe at first, but they soon see how their feedback helps them understand how today's leaders think. Indeed, there are no truly self-professed great listeners among leaders. Great listeners rely on others to affirm their skills.

During the pandemic, the sheer amount of information that needed to be heard, read, and digested by scientists, public health officials, medical professionals, public policymakers, regulators, customers, and the general public was staggering. Those of us in the medical diagnostic industry were initially unaccustomed to absorbing the volume, pace, complexity, interconnectedness, and dramatic changes in our daily information intake. On top of it all, versions of the truth, falsehoods, and plain old misdirection created background noise that overwhelmed reality at times. Making sense of it all and interpreting became key skills for leaders.

In their 2020 MIT Sloan Management Review article "The Overlooked Key to Leading through Chaos," Deborah Ancona, Michele Williams, and Gisela Gerlach assert that managers who focus on developing sensemaking capabilities can make better decisions in a complex and unpredictable world. Sensemaking is the ability to create and update maps of a complex environment to act more effectively in it. It involves pulling together disparate views to create a plausible understanding of the complexity around us and then testing that understanding to refine it or, if necessary, abandon it and start over. In other words, sensemaking helps leaders make better decisions by considering all of the relevant information. Few leaders model or implement sensemaking in their organizations, but research shows those who do are more successful.

These researchers view their findings as a call to action. "We must shift gears from assuming that we understand the world to being curious and experimenting, and from believing that sensemaking is required of only senior leaders to cultivating it at all levels of the organization. Rather than immediately jumping to solutions, we must start with collecting data and scrutinizing it for trends and patterns that point to better solutions; rather than ignoring warning signs of failure, we should learn from others what those warning signs might be. This is not the time to do less sensemaking—it is the time to supercharge your organization's ability to do more." Top leaders must role model sensemaking and help set the tone by thoughtfully interpreting information and teaching others to do so too.

For OraSure, the job of consciously choosing important facets of knowledge or clusters of insight and making them understandable, while presenting them even-handedly, began with me. We didn't name it sensemaking, but in effect, we practiced this type of interpreting. In October 2021, I wrote:

> If you're struggling to keep your inner peace during this pandemic, know that you're not alone. Here are some things that have helped me get through it:
>
> Accept that things are different right now and that they may never go back to exactly the way they were before.

Recognize the different aspects of grief that you may be feeling, such as loss, isolation, and uncertainty. Allow yourself to experience these emotions and reach out for support if needed.

Find activities, old or new, that fulfill you and bring you joy.

Focus on maintaining strong relationships with your loved ones. Lean on them for support and talk to them about your struggles.

Build regular practices into your life that promote resilience, such as getting enough sleep, eating well, exercising, meditating, being self-compassionate, and saying no when needed. Taking care of yourself is crucial during times of stress—make sure you're doing things that make you feel good physically and mentally. It will help you better understand and cope with your world.

Leaders need to model vulnerability in their interpreting process. This means being open to imperfection and acknowledging the limits of our understanding. By doing so, we can learn from experience and act accordingly. We must help people make sense not only of their work lives but also of the other aspects of their lives that were affected by the pandemic, such as isolation and loneliness. By modeling sensemaking, leaders can provide a valuable service to others who are struggling to make sense of their own lives in these difficult times.

OraSure's success during the pandemic can be attributed to our focus on the present and our ability to "mental time travel" to the past and future. The key to successful leadership is compassion, empowerment, accountability, engagement, and interpreting. Aligning the entire organization around its mission is crucial for empowering leaders and employees. Leaders need to treat others as equals and listen actively to learn from people to make sense of it all and share that information. Like much advice, it's easy to understand and difficult to deliver consistently and collectively. But for the next normal replete with unimaginable crises, we must aim to do so with skill and persistence.

Dear Steve…

———

"I appreciate the fact that you let the people who work for you live and grow through their mistakes and take on responsibility. I've learned more this year than probably any year in my professional career."

CHAPTER 5

Thriving

———

"Share with people who have earned the right to hear your story."
—BRENÉ BROWN, RESEARCHER, AUTHOR, AND SPEAKER
WHO STUDIES HUMAN CONNECTION AND VULNERABILITY

When Bill George urged leaders to be open and share their personal stories and vulnerabilities in his original printing of *True North* in 2007, most of the business world was just beginning to hear about vulnerability and authenticity. *Daring Greatly* and *The Power of Vulnerability* books by Brené Brown wouldn't appear until five years later. He may have been a misunderstood prophet in a hard-nosed business world back then.

Bill was correct that people feel empowered to share their own stories and uncertainties when leaders share their stories in ways that deeply connect with them. That leads to high engagement and alignment of interests and behaviors that enable organizations to achieve greatness. Companies with a culture of shared life stories naturally cultivate high trust fueled by high credibility and intimacy and resilience when encountering risk.

BALANCING VULNERABILITY AND POSITIVITY

When you share your personal story with others, it's important to find a balance between sharing too much information and too little. You don't want to overwhelm others with details, but you also don't want to seem like you're holding back. It's a delicate balance but one that can be achieved with thoughtfulness and intention. And when you do share your stories, be aware of the tone you're using. Are you being positive and uplifting, or are you coming across as negative and complaining? Most of all, you want to avoid "toxic positivity" that glosses over your struggles and makes others feel like they can't relate to you. Instead, strive for a healthy balance of vulnerability and positivity.

Toxic positivity is a problem because it dismisses negative emotions and instead offers false reassurances. This can be harmful because it doesn't allow people to process their feelings properly. High employee engagement requires emotional commitment by employees based on authentic feelings. Nothing less will do. Instead of toxic positivity, I suggest "tragic optimism." This involves searching for meaning amid the tragedies of life. It's more realistic and practical, and it can lead to personal growth. So, next time you're faced with a difficult situation, don't try to just put a positive spin on it. Instead, look for the meaning in it—even if it's gloomy—and use it as an opportunity to grow yourself and others.

I learned to embrace authentic sharing and tragic optimism because I felt bittersweetness deeply in my mind, heart, and soul during the pandemic. As Susan Cain writes in her book *Bittersweet*, "Bittersweetness is the hidden source of our moonshots, masterpieces, and love stories" (Cain 2022, xxvii). She believes we experience our deepest states of love, happiness, awe, and creativity precisely because life is imperfect, not despite it. At the heart of her exploration is the naming and reframing of her titular paradox: that there is no bitter without sweet.

I drew on that paradox many times as I shared my life stories with my OraSure colleagues. In my one hundred or so weekly Monday Motivational Messages from April 2020 to March 2022, I covered topics from moms, dads, graduations, and music to first jobs, religion, books, libraries, and many others. Each of them elicited sharing from my colleagues widely dispersed by job title and location. Many were poignant recollections about their own lives. Some were lighter fare that still amuse me.

These shared narratives were a form of time travel when actual travel was or seemed dangerous or unavailable. They transported us all to fond memories of people, places, and times that were more joyful and free than the bleakness of our shut-in, shutdown, and shutoff lives avoiding the coronavirus. Like mood-altering slingshots, they loaded us with goodness dipped from the past and then careened us into the future with hope.

Looking back, I see how my focus on the bittersweet aspects of life helped create a space for others to do the same. In a world that often tells us to just "be positive," embracing the full range of our emotions can be revolutionary. It can also be healing, connective, and transformative. So, the next time you're feeling down, don't try to force yourself to snap out of your gloom. Instead, allow yourself to feel all of your emotions and see what comes up for you. You might be surprised by what you find.

Sharing parts of my life also led to widespread support for and engagement in company initiatives for diversity, equity, and inclusion (DE&I) and mentorship. These initiatives helped us become better people and colleagues while growing our careers. Sharing my stories required me to recall and examine portions of my life I hadn't dwelled on for a while. Some were quite painful. The following four messages catalyzed the programs.

FITTING IN

The first addresses my childhood experience of "fitting in" as a kid of color. Because so few minorities are CEOs of public companies today, I realized I had the rare opportunity to speak about my experiences with prejudice and alienation. During my formative years in the 1960s and 1970s, I was often one of the only kids of color in any room or space I entered. I rarely had time to feel the warm embrace of belonging. Instead, my fight, flight, or freeze instincts were always activated. Back in those days, the notion of "belonging" was a bridge too far. Just fitting in seemed hard enough.

At any given moment, I could be called *chink*, *gook*, or *nip* and subject to ridicule and fights just for wearing my race on my face and minding my own business. My body often felt like adrenaline was constantly coursing through my veins. My heart seemed to always beat fast. I had to be ready to respond to indignities and take and give punches, anywhere and anytime. In an era defined by Black and white tensions, who cared about a solitary Asian kid just trying to fit in? I often felt alone.

> Being different as a kid is hard. Playing baseball taught me to persevere no matter what people say or think and to remain true to myself. Playing on teams that went from worst to first and won league championships, I learned how to earn the respect of my opponents, coaches, and teammates, how to tap into each player's strengths, and how interdependent we were as teammates.

> My baseball lessons stuck with me and have formed the foundation of my life's work to belong, lead, and elevate others in communities near and far. At the OraSure family of companies, we are diverse people of different races, religions, genders, sexual orientations, and nationalities. Yet every day I see examples of respect, loyalty, perseverance, and optimism. Together they make us who we are—a winning company. Let's celebrate the wins… and still strive to do better and be better people!

MODEL MINORITY MYTH

The second speaks to the thorny issue of the "model minority myth" for Asian Americans. Who knew prejudice and privilege could marry and spawn this wicked tale? So goes the story that Asians are white enough to not need special privileges like affirmative action, yet aren't white enough to be part of the mainstream majority. My family's history in the US as immigrants and as an assimilated minority is a cautionary tale embedded within the American Dream.

The model minority designation bestowed upon Asian Americans is a complicated one. On the one hand, it confirms the immigrant values of hard work, persistence, and independence that many in the community hold dear. On the other hand, it belies the discrimination and bias that Asian Americans often face, both from within and outside their vast community of different nationalities and languages. Adding to the complexity is that many of those incidences of Asian American Pacific Islander discrimination were from other minorities. So, it's more than a "white versus Asian" problem.

My grandfather first experienced this dichotomy when he arrived in Washington, DC, in 1946 to begin his job as an economist with the United Nations. He found a row house for his family near Catholic University, only to be told by the seller that he couldn't buy the home because he was Asian. Though my grandfather reminded the seller that China had been an ally of the United States during World War II, the seller was unconvinced. He feared backlash from his neighbors if it were revealed he had sold his home to someone who looked like they could be from Japan, America's former enemy.

What followed was a frustrating and even humiliating series of events in which my grandfather had to ask a white colleague to buy the home on his behalf and then sell it back to him later. This story is not unique, unfortunately. It's just one example of how minorities have long been discriminated against when it comes to housing and upward mobility.

It's no surprise, then, that Harvard University is currently being sued over its admissions policy, which allegedly discriminates against Asian American applicants. According to the lawsuit, Harvard gives Asian American applicants lower personal ratings, which are supposed to denote characteristics like leadership and grit. If true, that means it's harder for Asians to be admitted.

This type of discrimination is nothing new, but it's still just as harmful and hurtful as it ever was. That's why we need to have an honest and open dialog about diversity, equity, and inclusion in our society. Only then can we begin to move forward toward a more equitable future for all.

UNCONSCIOUS BIAS

The third addresses unconscious bias. Even with the scars of fitting in and living up to the model minority myth, I admit to still having bias. I've tried to make introspection, self-growth, and the intellectual curiosity that goes with them a priority in my life. Yet I still have a long way to go to have peace with my own bias.

When it comes to race, we all have personal biases that we may not even be aware of. I know I do. Growing up in a predominantly white community, I was mostly exposed to white culture and didn't have a lot of interaction with people of other racial backgrounds. As a result, I developed some unconscious biases against minorities.

It wasn't until I started working at OraSure, a small but truly global company with employees of all different races, that I began to realize the error of my ways. Through my interactions with my colleagues, I came to understand the importance of diversity and inclusion. I realized that we all have different experiences and perspectives that can enrich our lives and make us better people.

I also came to understand the importance of acknowledging our personal biases. We all have them, and they can shape our view of the world. By acknowledging our biases, we can begin to change them.

One way we can do this is by being more aware of the language we use. For example, certain backhanded compliments (like "You're beautiful for someone who has [insert physical or ethnic trait]") can have racist overtones. If we're not careful, these kinds of comments can perpetuate racial stereotypes.

We all must take the time to examine our own experiences with race and how they've shaped our beliefs about ourselves and others. Only then can we begin to move beyond racial bias and inequity. I know I'm still learning, but I'm committed to making progress. I hope you'll join me.

MENTORING

For the fourth, on mentoring, I drew from my own experiences and those of former US Secretary of State Condoleezza Rice. Once you've been mentored by an exceptional person, it becomes instinctual to give back and be receptive to others seeking your mentorship. I am fortunate to have been so graced.

I'm grateful to my former advisor, Arthur Humphrey, for everything he did for me during and after my PhD program. He not only helped me academically but also became a surrogate father figure and an influence on my life outside of academia. I remember when I was finishing up my doctorate and struggling with health issues that limited my physical activity. It would have been easy for Arthur to push me harder and expect more from me, but instead, he showed genuine concern for my well-being and helped me get through that difficult time.

After I graduated, Arthur continued to support me as I started my own technical consulting business and went back to school for an MBA. His guidance and advice have been invaluable in helping me achieve success in my career. I know that not everyone is lucky enough to have a mentor like Arthur in their life, but I believe everyone deserves one.

I've been fortunate to have many opportunities to serve as a mentor, sponsor, ally, and advocate for other people throughout my career. It's something that I take a lot of pride in because it's always gratifying to see someone I've mentored or supported succeed in their career. As part of OraSure's diversity, equity, and inclusion initiative, I'm hoping to see more mentoring relationships develop within our company so everyone has an opportunity to learn and grow. If we can achieve this, it will make us an even stronger and more resilient team.

I also encourage you to consider the words of former US Secretary of State Condoleezza Rice, who said, "Search for role models you can look up to and people who take an interest in your career. But here's an important warning: You don't have to have mentors who look like you. Had I been waiting for a Black, female Soviet specialist mentor, I would still be waiting. Most of my mentors have been old white men because they were the ones who dominated my field" (Tulshyan 2013). Secretary Rice and I are baby boomers who had limited opportunity to choose diversity in a mentor. Fortunately, we've come far at OraSure, with many women and people of color who could serve as mentors.

That piece triggered an avalanche of replies with great ideas for OraSure's mentoring program.

COLLECTIVE EFFERVESCENCE

So, how did an undersized, pandemic-challenged company founded in an underdog community break through to create InteliSwab and transform itself? We did it by first surviving and making the health, safety, and well-being of our people the nonnegotiable priority. We acknowledged that isolation and loneliness take their toll on our physical, mental, and spiritual health and provided programs and guidance to encourage everyone to seek professional care and self-care.

Once we had established trust between us, we were able to blossom and reach heights we hadn't previously dreamed of. With this strong foundation, we were able to unlock greater potential and create something extraordinary. While not everyone was flourishing at the same time because of the individual struggles each of us faced, we did reach "collective effervescence." The shared enthusiasm for our DE&I and mentoring programs had a lot do with reaching this state of triumph.

Collective effervescence is a sociological concept coined by Émile Durkheim, a French sociologist at the turn of the twentieth century (Renz 2021). According to Durkheim, a community or society may, at times, come together and simultaneously communicate the same thought and participate in the same action. Like a crowd cheering madly for its team to win and losing itself in celebration once victory is at hand, we navigated big and small crises, unforeseen pivots, and thorny technical problems together. Enabled by leadership ethos based on compassion, empowerment, accountability, and engagement, we pulled together for our common cause of extracting our fellow humans—and ourselves—from the confines of the pandemic.

Dear Steve...

———

"Thank you for your leadership and for not being afraid to show us the human side of you that we typically don't see with people in your position."

CHAPTER 6

Twilight Zone

———

"There's far more here than meets the eye. The things we see now are here today, gone tomorrow. But the things we can't see now will last forever."

—2 CORINTHIANS 4:18, MSG

And then, it all abruptly ended for me at OraSure.

In the four years between 2018 and 2022, OraSure acquired more companies and launched more products than ever before. We also expanded our global presence, commissioned new facilities, nearly doubled our workforce, and rapidly increased our manufacturing capacity. Despite all this success, I said goodbye to OraSure. During my time at the helm, OraSure stock price had a higher average daily closing value than under any previous CEO. I'm proud of what we accomplished during my time as a leader and hope the company will continue to thrive. So far, so good. They have continued to report record quarterly revenue throughout 2022 and improved profitability, as I anticipated at my departure.

As CEO, it was my job to set reasonable expectations with investment banks' sell-side research analysts. These analysts then provide customers with a view of our future quarterly performance. The average of all these predictions is known as "consensus." Beating consensus typically triggers buying from investors, while missing it can often lead to a selloff. In today's world of automated exchanges and investors who decide by algorithm, beats, misses, or meets are vital to the stock price and investor confidence.

Since 2011, when I joined OraSure's board of directors, the company had a mixed record with performance versus consensus. We had some beats, some misses, and some meets. This continued during my tenure as CEO. During the pandemic, many companies found it difficult to predict their quarterly results due to a variety of issues, many related to the uncertainty caused by lockdowns, supply chain disruptions, and changing customer demand. Some companies decided to suspend guidance altogether, leaving analysts to pick their own numbers. This often led to consensus based on widely divergent views. Adding to the challenges were frequent spikes upward and downward for the stock market as a whole, which is called volatility. Predicting quarterly performance by professionals or amateurs was not for the faint of heart.

I took my job seriously and devoted my time and effort to stewarding shareholder value. In addition to me, the chief financial officer and investor relations team worked closely with the board's audit committee to review and approve guidance to "the street." That way, everyone was assured we evaluated the numbers with as much scrutiny as possible.

All other senior executives participated in this discussion to ensure there was complete alignment between the company's leadership and board.

KNOWING WHAT YOU DON'T KNOW

When OraSure was getting ready to sell massive amounts of its new InteliSwab product, we had to make some big changes so we could produce the product on a larger scale than the company had achieved before. Lisa Nibauer knew what needed to get done because she had led similar expansions in her assignments before OraSure. However, one person's experience—no matter how profound—wasn't sufficient to infuse capability across an entire company, which is especially true when the requirements for quickly scaling up manufacturing touched so many people in so many functions to ensure high quality and regulatory compliance. Few organizations have the self-awareness of their limitations while so much is happening so fast every day.

The challenge of "knowing what we don't know" and taking action on it can be daunting. It's tempting to stay comfortable with established methods and habits, especially when they've been successful in the past. But for ambitious organizations like ours, striving for a Mars Mission, it's critical to keep learning and looking for opportunities—even if that means failing at times. After all, failure often teaches us the most valuable lessons.

In this case, Lisa Nibauer was able to lead OraSure through a successful launch and expansion of InteliSwab, even after

I left. But every organization needs to take heed that it's important to anticipate capability gaps and organizational inertia challenges before they happen.

MY FAILURES

Looking back on it all, many aspects of this manufacturing expansion plan could have gone better. I consider that my biggest failure. Here's an example of where my high accountability and empowerment approach needed additional features for this enormous challenge, and I admit it. I needed more than Lisa's oracle "voice crying out in the wilderness" to address the massive step-up in our manufacturing capacity. I needed a legion of "been there, done that" insurgents hired much sooner in our journey. Fortunately, our setbacks proved to be temporary and were ultimately resolved through new hires, hard work, tenacity, and wisdom.

My second biggest failure was permitting the company to publicly announce our intended target manufacturing capacity for InteliSwab, which ultimately created expectations that we couldn't meet later in 2021 and into 2022. This created a lot of pressure on the company that could have been avoided if we had handled things differently. Learning from these failures was essential in helping OraSure get back on track and meet the high demand for its product, which it did by mid-2022.

Manufacturing problems for COVID-19 tests were noteworthy across our industry throughout the pandemic. Abbott's BinaxNOW—the biggest selling self-test on the market—was in limited supply after they shut down a manufacturing plant and then restarted it as demand for testing dramatically increased in the summer of 2021 due to the Delta and Omicron variants. Cue Health rose from startup obscurity to fame as the provider of tests for the National Basketball Association and advertiser on Super Bowl commercials, only to repeatedly miss their production obligations for a 481-million-dollar federal government contract. They were eventually excluded from similar government contracts and laid off many people.

ACTIVIST INVESTORS

An activist investor buys a significant stake in a public company to influence how the business is run. Their goal is to buy stocks they view as undervalued and pressure management to do things they believe will raise the company's stock price. Like many companies during the pandemic, OraSure's share price ran up and down often as investors sorted through information about the company and the broader stock market that was often conflicting and nebulous. In the rollercoaster and shark-tooth descriptions of our stock price I've shared previously, many causes for those movements were within our control and some were not.

By November 2021, an activist investor announced in a US Securities and Exchange Commission filing that they had bought a big enough stake in OraSure to be considered an activist and informed the board of their intentions. The board then initiated a "strategic review," which is typically a process to seek potential buyers and calibrate the value of the company. At the same time, they launched a CEO search process for my successor.

As Bill George and Jay W. Lorsch explain in their *Harvard Business Review* article "How to Outsmart Activist Investors," activist investors tend to target companies to divide their boards (2014). To deal with these issues practically and impartially, directors must nurture and maintain board chemistry, which can be achieved over time through dialogue regarding important matters, working collaboratively through crises, and cultivating transparency from the CEO so critical information is shared. To effectively handle any pressure from activists, directors need to be fully devoted to the company's long-term aims, even during times when the stock price is under pressure. I thought I had done my part to foster cohesion within board, but apparently it wasn't enough.

I kept the board updated with weekly reports as soon as the pandemic started. I did so to ensure clear transparency and timely communication. Their feedback was strongly positive, encouraging, and supportive. One board member pointed out to me that the depth and timeliness of the information I shared was truly exceptional compared to other CEOs during this time. I worked diligently and intentionally to ensure there were no surprises for the board. Even so, CEOs always serve at the pleasure of their boards who reserve the right to change CEOs at any time. As most top executive employment contracts stipulate, CEOs can be terminated without cause. It's part of the job that we all accept, albeit with some degree of angst.

CEOS SERVE SELFLESSLY

By stepping down, I had hoped the stock price would rebound and benefit all of those involved. The board certainly thought so as well, considering the headline from the company's January 5, 2022, press release announcing my departure, "OraSure Technologies Announces Actions to Enhance Shareholder Value." As a significant shareholder in the company and along with many others, I continue to wish them well in that pursuit.

Many executives put others' interests before themselves during the pandemic. Examples such as Yvon Chouinard of Patagonia, who committed to keeping his employees paid during the coronavirus pandemic crisis despite store closures, have demonstrated the positive effects proactive leadership can have on both organizations and individuals alike. Similarly, executives from Hearst, LinkedIn, Morgan Stanley, and other companies put their financial interests aside to ensure staff was protected during these challenging times. This act of putting others before oneself is something that should be celebrated and replicated throughout the business world.

By showing my commitment to putting others before myself, particularly during a time of great uncertainty, I hope I have set an example for others to follow. Only through collective selflessness can we help our companies and communities survive trying times. Trust based on credibility and intimacy must overwhelm risks and remains the basis for cohesion during such crises.

MAKING SENSE OF IT ALL THROUGH CHRISTMAS GHOSTS

Because of my separation agreement with the company, I can't comment further about the circumstances surrounding my departure. What I can share is that this was a devastating experience for my family and me. As you can imagine, this situation put a serious damper on Jill's and my celebration of her year-long recovery from her near-fatal fall. In the blur of events coinciding with the year-end holidays, I sought perspective on my plight. It came to me in a classic holiday story.

A Christmas Carol serves as an example of how important it is for leaders today to be mindful of their actions and the impact they can have on others. It can be easy for busy professionals to get caught up in day-to-day operations, but ultimately taking time to show compassion and kindness will lead to better relationships with employees, customers, and partners alike. *A Christmas Carol* shows us that leaders can learn and grow from their mistakes, just like Scrooge did. By recognizing our potential for transformation, enlightened leaders can take the lessons from the ghosts of Christmas past, present, and future to create prosperous businesses that have a positive impact on society.

To help me cope and make sense of my situation, I looked to examples of those who sought forgiveness, dignity, and humor.

CHOOSE FORGIVENESS AND SEEK DIGNITY

When Nelson Mandela was sentenced to life in prison for his role in ending apartheid in South Africa, he could have easily become resentful and angry. But instead, he chose to forgive his captors and work toward a better future. After twenty-seven years in prison, Mandela was released and became the leader of the African National Congress party. He went on to become the first Black president of South Africa. Rather than taking revenge on his opponents, Mandela worked to cooperate with them. He brought several of his fiercest rivals into the government and even invited one of his prison guards to the presidential inauguration.

Mandela's decision to forgive rather than seek revenge is an example of how powerful forgiveness can be. It's a reminder that no matter how difficult our circumstances may be, we always have the choice to respond with dignity. And when we do, we open the door to a brighter future for us all.

GALLOWS HUMOR

Months after my departure, I had a gallows humor moment when I learned about how the board of directors of Men's Wearhouse fired George Zimmer in 2013 after forty years of service. John B. Stewart covered the story for the Longwood (Texas) News-Journal on November 29, 2015. Zimmer was the founder and public face of the retail chain Men's Wearhouse. "You're going to like the way you look. I guarantee it" was their motto. The lead director called him in and said,

"You're terminated. We're packing up your office furniture and putting it in storage," Zimmer recalled.

His ouster came as a personal blow, especially since he counted some of the directors among his closest friends. That included famed author and new-age guru Deepak Chopra. According to Zimmer, Chopra led him through a guided meditation soon before the firing. Said Zimmer, "I didn't think a man of his elevated consciousness would care about an extra nickel for shareholders, but he didn't support me." Now that's sardonic humor under duress.

My *Twilight Zone* ending journey at OraSure opened my eyes to the life-altering gifts of grace, honor, and laughter—may they stay with me always. The experience taught me the significance of viewing reality through clear eyes, without the filter of assumptions or expectations.

Dear Steve…

"You should be proud of the way you've led and the integrity you brought to your role every day. You've done a ton for the company in terms of reinvigorating innovation, helping us through some real challenges with the pandemic, and getting the company ready to grow and scale in size. The company got unlucky with a few setbacks, but otherwise we are much better positioned for the next five years."

CHAPTER 7

Wounded Healers

———

"The ultimate measure of a leader's success is that they leave those who follow in their footsteps with the determination and motivation to keep going."
—PARAPHRASED FROM WALTER LIPPMAN, AMERICAN WRITER, REPORTER, AND POLITICAL COMMENTATOR

Buddha taught us that the root of suffering is attachment because the only constant in the universe is change. This is also a key concept in Christian spirituality, where it signifies a detachment from worldly objects and concerns. I admit I suffered deeply after December 2021 because I was attached to a fantasy end to my tenure at OraSure. However, I have realized this attachment caused me more suffering than anything else. By detaching myself, I've found some peace and acceptance.

A CEO's last hundred days before leaving their position usually can be split up into three phases: preannouncement, post-announcement, and pre-transition. How an organization and individuals handle these phases is crucial to having a smooth transition and keeping the company running. For the CEO leaving their position, it is important to maintain good relationships with others in the industry as well as a positive reputation. Nearly all departing CEOs want to end their time with the company on a high note, and I certainly was one of them.

WOUNDED HEALERS RISE UP

Despite all my turmoil, I began to play a new role as a "wounded healer" for the people of OraSure in January 2022. I didn't have time to dwell on my own disappointment. As author Douglas C. Smith describes in his book *Being a Wounded Healer* (1999), "Accepting our own woundedness is the key to our own healing; and it opens up our ability to show others congruence, empathy, and unconditional positive regard; hence, assisting them in their healing." This meant I needed to leave my employees and my board with what psychologist Carl Rogers calls three "conditions for growth," namely:

1. Congruence (authenticity, honesty, vulnerability; including our woundedness).
2. Empathy (feeling and experiencing another's suffering as if it were our own).
3. Unconditional positive regard (accepting, loving, and valuing a person as-is, even with their hurts, scars, wounds, and imperfections).

When we share our wounds, we also share in each other's healing. By sharing our personal growth and strengths, we give each other hope. We show each other it is possible to live and grow despite our wounds and, more importantly, because of our wounds. We also show each other that we are not alone in this journey. We need each other; we help each other. And when we heal, we heal each other.

The healing began with my departure announcement in a Zoom meeting on January 5, 2022. Here's what I shared with them as I choked back tears, breaking my composure several times, and pausing often to collect myself:

> I will be leaving the company at the end of March. I'll be staying on until that time to assist in the CEO transition and lead the strategic review initiative. CEO transitions are big news in companies like ours. I was part of OraSure's last CEO transition announcement, almost four years ago to the day. While I'm sad to be leaving, I am confident that under OraSure's next era of leadership, the company will be well-positioned to take advantage of the opportunities ahead. Please know that, from the bottom of my heart and soul, it's been the honor and privilege of my career to be your colleague and work closely with you. I've grown to love our work together and genuinely love each of you for who you are, what you do, the ways you've supported each other, and how you've endured this pandemic.

A few days later, I called for healing when I wrote:

> It can be easy to feel overwhelmed by the constant stream of change and uncertainty in the world. But it's important to remember we are all in this together. We are stronger when we work together and support each

other. I've been so impressed by the way everyone at OraSure has pulled together during this pandemic. Because our leadership team remains highly empowered and accountable, they will enable us to continue meeting the challenges ahead.

Another theme I've been thinking about a lot lately is "nothing stands alone." Theologian and author Kate Bowler shares this view: "It's hard to remember a deeper, comforting truth: We are built on a foundation not our own," she says. "We were born because two other people created a combination of biological matter. We went to schools where dozens and dozens of people crafted ideas and activities to construct categories in our minds. We learned skills honed by generations of craftspeople. We pray and worship with spiritual ideas refined by centuries of tradition. Almost nothing about us is original."

I find this perspective fascinating, and it makes me consider that we need each other more now than ever before. During my remaining three months at OraSure, I will strongly advocate this message and reiterate our need for teamwork.

I've been overwhelmed by the many messages you've sent to me following Wednesday's announcements. Please know I've been rereading and reflecting on each of them and will respond to each of you in the coming weeks. Thank you for your support during this time of transition. I know that together we will continue to build an even stronger OraSure.

Seeing hundreds of people from every corner of the organization determined to take up our cause even in my absence was a remarkable sight to behold. I received an outpouring of empathy, compassion, and raw emotion in the form of heartfelt letters. Among them was one moving passage from one of many wounded healers dedicated to advancing our mission without me.

Dear Steve...

———

"A heart full of love just for you... We have worked together but not closely for the last four years. I can't begin to tell you the impact your commitment to conscious leadership has had on my life and the lives of those I am so blessed to lead. That's the true success story here. The products and the impact they have had on society matter, no doubt. However, fostering the environment for love/growth/accountability—that's the real game changer."

CHAPTER 8

Lead Whole People Wholeheartedly!

———

"A leader... is like a shepherd. He stays behind the flock, letting the most nimble go out ahead, whereupon the others follow, not realizing that all along they are being directed from behind."

—NELSON MANDELA, ANTI-APARTHEID ACTIVIST
AND FIRST BLACK PRESIDENT OF SOUTH AFRICA

What could have been a fragile destiny for OraSure became a story of strength and growth through struggle, thanks to the company's embrace of chaos and mayhem. There's even an odd word for it—antifragile. If you ask most people, "What's the opposite of fragile?" I would imagine that many would say "strong" or "resilient." Those are good answers, but there's a succinct one—"antifragile."

I wasn't aware that antifragile was a thing until I read the 2012 book by Nassim Nicholas Taleb called *Antifragile: Things That Gain from Disorder* (2012), which reveals how to thrive in an uncertain and unsettled world. Just as human bones get stronger when subjected to stress and tension, which is how exercise helps us, many things in life benefit from stress, disorder, volatility, and turmoil. What Taleb calls "antifragile" is that category of things that not only gain from chaos and mayhem but need it to survive and flourish.

Taleb stands pandemonium on its head, making it desirable, even necessary, and proposes that things be built in an antifragile manner. Unlike resiliency, which resists shocks and stays the same, the antifragile absorbs shocks and gets better and better. OraSure is a perfect example of an antifragile company. It has thrived amid uncertainty and chaos, gaining strength from the stress and turmoil it has faced. In a world that is ever-changing and unpredictable, embracing the antifragile mindset is essential for success.

Amid the COVID-19 pandemic, OraSure became antifragile by pulling together teams to deliver high-quality, innovative work. Despite the stresses and shocks of the pandemic, we grew and strengthened our ranks, all while serving humanity with InteliSwab—the easiest-to-use COVID-19 home test of its kind. Oprah Winfrey's company even endorsed our product! We learned to trust each other as the foundation for surviving, cared for each other as the core of aligning our mission, and grew to be a bigger, stronger company that helped tame the coronavirus through a product based on a near effortless testing experience for customers.

A CARING CULTURE HAS NO WALLS

We often think about care as respect for our work and each other, as in "I care deeply about my work." It used to be something that happens in an office or some other professional setting that requires us to be physically present. But the pandemic forced us to reevaluate what it means to be caring. Care is not just respect—it's more like love and the effort and choices that go into love—nor is it confined to any one place. Care can happen anywhere, anytime, with anyone.

A caring culture is present in our homes, on walks and hikes, in music and art, and on the faces we see on video calls. It's with us when we're feeling overwhelmed by work or online school. And it's with us when we're praying for the sick and injured in hospitals.

COVID-19 has shown us that a caring culture doesn't just happen in buildings. It happens anywhere two, three, or more people are gathered—even if it's just you and your pets at home. It's in the bread we bake and bless at our quarantine family tables. As CEO, I didn't amp up the wholehearted caring culture at OraSure. The pandemic did. I simply noticed and nurtured it.

One day, all buildings will reopen, but many people will not go back to them. They'll stay home for at least part of the workweek because they've discovered they can be just as caring about their work and people outside of an office setting. The pandemic may have hastened this process for some, but for others, it was just a matter of asking new questions about their values or renewing their courage on their career journey.

Many others will return to work in classrooms, stores, restaurants, hotels, office buildings, warehouses, factories, laboratories, farms, oil rigs, coal mines, and other places. As we did before, people will sit close, chat at the proverbial water cooler, and hug and share snacks and meals. Whatever happens, I hope the people of OraSure will remember the caring culture we experienced during a time of fear and confusion. It's based on our shared experiences. It mattered then and matters now.

I'm not a scholar or theorist who offers grand, all-encompassing explanations for everything. I'm a long-time practitioner of leadership who has seen firsthand how worlds can change when people, organizations, power, and circumstances align. I share my thoughts in the hope that the next generation of would-be Mark Watneys marooned in their bases on some distant planet can learn from our OraSure experience and science more shit out of their situation than we were able to.

A NEXT NORMAL REPLETE WITH CRISES

COVID-19 will likely be with us for many more years. Trevor Bedford, a computational virologist at the Fred Hutchinson Cancer Center in Seattle, said in a July 20, 2022, *New York Times* opinion piece by David Wallace-Wells that we can expect every year, around 50 percent of Americans will be infected and more than one hundred thousand will die.

Bedford said, "A hundred thousand deaths is more than the annual toll of any other infectious disease and would make COVID-19 a top-ten cause of death in the country—a major and novel cause of widespread death clouding the American horizon with another dark layer of morbidity we had never known before" (Wallace-Wells 2022). That's chilling, and it gets more fraught if we think about a world with other ominous emerging trends, both natural and man-made.

There will undoubtedly be other crises that test our resolve. With climate change causing ecosystem shifts, it's only a matter of time before we see more viruses like COVID-19, Ebola, and Mpox jumping between species. Viruses don't discriminate. They'll take advantage of any opportunity to invade the human species. And with extreme weather, social unrest, political strife, economic downturns and inequality, wars, and geopolitical power struggles on the rise, "unforeseen circumstances" are becoming more and more common. As a result, even the best-laid plans can be easily disrupted.

In The Conference Board's 2022 CEO survey, they asked leaders to identify the biggest business challenges for the year ahead. The results revealed that fewer than 40 percent of CEOs believe they are well-prepared to handle a major crisis related to challenges such as inflation, recession, cybersecurity, supply chain disruptions, or climate change—much less all of them at the same time. I would expect survey numbers to decline for 2023 with more uncertainty and potential threats on the horizon.

This stunning revelation shines the spotlight on the pressing need to prepare people, organizations, and communities to survive and thrive. But are we already too overwhelmed with the present to deal with the onslaught of crises in the next normal? Maybe so, yet it is the duty of all leaders to be prepared, which means our approach to identifying opportunities, developing capabilities, and addressing the unknown need to be better honed now.

So, what can we do to be better prepared for the next normal? We need to take a step back and assess what we are doing now and how we can improve. We also need to be honest about our limitations and what we can realistically handle. Only then can we develop a plan that will help us flourish in the face of innumerable crises.

VIGILANCE AND ADJUSTMENT

We all have a hard time seeing problems coming until it's too late. The reason is we're busy with our own lives and might not pay attention to warning signs, or we might not be curious enough to investigate them. We all need to be more aware of what's happening around us so we can avoid disasters. I know I've been guilty of this myself, whether it's misreading early signals from activist shareholders, waiting too long to address manufacturing scale-up plans, or managing expectations for our projected InteliSwab capacity.

As we absorb social media and other noise-making sources of questionable information, we may frame troubling issues in overly abstract—and easier to dismiss—terms, losing touch with what matters. We also may not appreciate the stresses others are under or the reasons they may withhold information from us. The net result is a partial and often distorted view of what is happening right under our noses.

When we are vigilant, we focus our attention to create greater agility and mastery. When we are defenseless, our misdirected attention creates blind spots, myopia, and delayed reactions. The challenge for us all is to deal appropriately with vast amounts of seemingly "regular" information while strengthening our ability to pay closer attention to what matters most.

Over the past few years, we've learned that we need our companies, organizations, and communities to be aligned, allied, and strongly connected to magnify our focus and minimize distractions. Accomplishing this is the profound challenge of leadership for the next normal replete with crises. It begins by empowering people, as well as welcoming and adjusting to differences in working styles. In September 2020, I wrote about the leader's role in recognizing and optimizing individual work-life preferences for those working remotely.

> It's no secret that we all have different preferences for how and when we get our work done. Wharton Professor Nancy Rothbard (2022) highlights the difference between "integrators," people who are comfortable blurring the boundary between work and home, and "segmentors," people who want a clear separation between their personal and professional lives. Both have their strengths, and managers need to be aware of these differences to capitalize on them effectively.

Integrators tend to be more flexible with their work hours and don't mind working outside of the traditional nine to five. On the other hand, segmentors prefer a more structured workday and might not be as open to working odd hours. As a leader, it's important to consider these differences and be respectful of people's preferences.

One way to help manage these differences is by communicating with your team and negotiating schedules that work for everyone. For example, if you're a segmentor working from home, you might want to create a schedule and routines to help structure your time. This will help you transition into and out of work mode more easily.

Keep in mind that it's important to be flexible and aware that what works for you might not work for everyone else on the team. By being open-minded and understanding different work styles, you can create a more harmonious workplace.

End-of-work rituals can also help those who work onsite transition to home life. When a firefighter in one of Professor Rothbard's studies, a segmentor, ends his shift, he puts on flip-flops to avoid bringing his firefighting boots into his house, takes a shower, and changes his clothes before hugging his wife and children.

Right now, I'm hard at work from home, but I look forward to a run or bike ride at the beginning of the day to clear my mind before diving into the work-day. I don't have an end-the-day ritual, because the workday doesn't always have a tidy ending for this integrator. What strategies work for you? I'd love to hear them.

I heard from many people about their work preferences and how they were dealing with challenges between segmentors and integrators. If the company could help them with furniture, equipment, or technology, we did so. If they needed to address differences with supervisors or colleagues, we convened those discussions. In all cases, my role was to listen, acknowledge, validate, and empathize with their concerns. We all need to appreciate that the skills to manage and lead people—many of whom were working remotely—weren't taught to or experienced by most of us until March 13, 2020, the day the pandemic lockdown began.

MY BIGGEST LESSON LEARNED

If I had to sum up my most profound takeaway from crisis leadership during the pandemic, it would be:

Lead whole people wholeheartedly!

No matter where you are on your journey toward survival and thriving, nor the type and magnitude of crises you face, leading people with compassion, accountability, empowerment, and engagement while welcoming their *entire being*—not just as workers tasked with jobs—breeds vigilance, adaptability, and learning for any next normal ahead of us.

When it comes to wholehearted leadership, being nice isn't nearly enough. We need to be both compassionate and wise. Wisdom, in this context, refers to a deep understanding of what motivates people and how to manage them so they deliver on agreed priorities. To be effective leaders, we must be able to navigate the tension between being caring and thoughtful and holding people to high standards. This requires openness and active listening so we can understand the unique circumstances of each team member.

Make it clear what is required for the job while also taking into account each team member's circumstances. We need to encourage team members to hold each other accountable. Accountability can be a collective goal, and it works best when the whole team is committed to it, not just select individuals. Be realistic about what you can and can't do for people as their leader. Done right, *accountability is an investment in results, and compassion is an investment in people*—both of which are necessary under the best and worst of conditions.

CEO AS PASTOR

If we want to lead whole people wholeheartedly, we need to revisit our role models for CEOs. Maybe it's time to check into how CEOs behave like pastors, recalling that, in many languages, pastor means shepherd. Just as a pastor is held accountable for the performance of their congregation or flocks, regardless of where any fault may lie, so, too, is a CEO blamed by shareholders if desired rewards aren't forthcoming. The best CEOs are also servant leaders who get things done by serving and empowering others rather than using force.

The CEO also sets the moral tone for the corporation. No matter how many mission statements or codes of conduct a company may have, top leadership sets the example. Furthermore, CEOs often have to do a lot of hand-holding and share leadership with others. If they are wise, they will delegate and share responsibility rather than try to do everything themselves. In short, CEOs could learn a lot from pastors about how to effectively lead people.

Just as pastors see their work as an assignment from the divine, so, too, could CEOs view their work as a calling from the universe. By doing so, they can ensure they are always looking out for the best interests of their employees, no matter where they are located. If CEOs and other leaders could commit to these pastoral practices, work design challenges such as remote versus hybrid versus office-based wouldn't be so perplexing and distressing.

When leaders are afraid of failure, they retreat to familiar ways of operating instead of being bold and experimental, which can lead them to become less empathetic to what others want and ultimately hinder their productivity. We've seen this dilemma with working from home. Working from home can be productive, but it requires a different approach than working in an office. When people work from home, they need to be more self-motivated and organized. They also need to find ways to stay connected with their team, whether that's through video calls or other means. Before the pandemic, conventional wisdom predicted that worker productivity would suffer greatly because of work-from-home practices.

In OraSure's experience, this simply wasn't true. If anything, our challenge was managing burnout from people working too hard without healthy boundaries to get InteliSwab and other products made and out to customers. I attribute our success to a pastoral approach to leadership.

CEO AS DRAGOMAN

A CEO could also be a dragoman. The ancient dragoman was a translator who often held immense power and political sway. Being a dragoman was not for the faint of heart because language translation and diplomacy during a crisis was a risky business. In the nineteenth century, when the UK and Russia were competing for control of Central Asia, Britain's and Russia's respective translators were hacked to death.

While today's CEOs may not suffer similarly violent fates, they need to work behind the scenes to bridge the understanding gap between leaders in siloed disciplines and roles. Those skills will play a crucial role in solving the multiple challenges the crises present in the next normal. In our fragmenting, albeit globalized world, cultural understanding is key. Dragomen have skills that are vital for the future workplace, including empathy, relationship management, adaptability, and teamwork.

There's a strong case for CEOs and other leaders to use cultural translation skills to deal with all sorts of crises—from technological and diplomatic challenges to shareholder and employee expectations. Dragomen are excellent at making sense of complex situations and choosing what to say and when to say it based on a deep understanding of the different agendas at play. The best dragomen were said to have created the illusion that no language or cultural barrier existed between opposing parties while they were conversing.

Pastors and dragomen are important role models to navigate unfamiliar territory. They can help interpret the local customs and language, and they can provide a valuable connection to and within the company. Pastors interpret faith and offer guidance and comfort. Dragomans act as guides and interpreters for sojourners and pilgrims. By acting as such mediators, CEOs can help prevent misunderstandings and conflict to better advocate for aligned missions.

FOCUS ON STAKEHOLDERS, NOT JUST SHAREHOLDERS

As a leader, it's important to take care of all those within our charge. This means considering the needs of employees, customers, and other stakeholders when making decisions—not just shareholders. Shareholders may own part of a company, but they don't have the same vested interest in its long-term success as those who work for or are served by the business.

It's time to create a system of capitalism that puts human beings first. Not only is it the right thing to do, but it's also good for business. Prioritizing the needs of employees, customers, and other stakeholders will lead to a stronger, more successful company in the long run.

A company's board of directors needs to have a clear understanding of stakeholder versus shareholder governance to assess the demands of activist shareholders with a keen perspective and objectivity without haste or panic. Not all shareholders are equal in their interest and intent in buying their shares. Hedge funds, for example, are notorious "share renters" who can make money even when a company's share price declines through short sales (i.e., borrowing stock at one price and paying for it at a lower price once the price declines) or options to buy or sell the stock at specific prices. In doing so, they can and do treat companies as rental cars, without the care that a long-term owner would have.

Simon Sinek, renowned author and leadership mensch, when asked during an *Inc. Magazine* podcast on July 2020, warned that boards without understanding or discernment of their shareholder base can act like "a coach who's trying to build a great team taking advice from the fans rather than listening to the players." Boards who chose to listen to fans who claimed they were loyal ticketholders and deserved a seat at the board table be forewarned.

More likely, these "fans" figuratively bought their tickets from the equivalent of a ticket reseller and made money selling off the stock as it plunged to lower prices. Tragically, the truly loyal shareholders—think of them as season ticketholders in this analogy—also sold off large portions of their holdings during this time, resulting in the team's "fanbase" being obliterated quickly and unnecessarily.

Such is the cautionary tale for boards who need to declare themselves as either stakeholder or shareholder governing but don't and are then forced to make bad decisions that aren't in the long-term interest of the ecosystem supporting the company. Even boards that declare themselves as catering only to shareholders need to be more aware of and discerning about which shareholders are most valuable to them.

Only then can they properly evaluate and objectively respond to activists and weigh the effect actions will have on the desirable and valuable shareholders. I deeply believe stakeholder governance is in the best interest of long-term shareholders—a view shared by pastors and dragomen, I'm sure.

Shareholders may own part of a company, but they don't have the same vested interest in its long-term success as those who work for or are served by the business. In today's business landscape, it's more important than ever for CEOs to take a stand for what they believe is right for their employees, customers, and other stakeholders—even if it means going against the wishes of shareholders. By taking this approach, leaders can build resilient people and prosperous companies that will last for years to come.

Dear Steve...

"I will forever be a better leader, person, son, father, grandfather, mentee, and mentor because of you and the examples and lessons you imparted."

CHAPTER 9

Next Normal

"Resilience is accepting your new reality, even if it's less good than the one you had before. You can fight it, you can do nothing but scream about what you've lost, or you can accept that and try to put together something that's good."

—ELIZABETH EDWARDS, AMERICAN ATTORNEY,

AUTHOR, AND HEALTH CARE ACTIVIST

The terms "new normal" and "next normal" are often used interchangeably, but they have different meanings. The new normal refers to the current pandemic-era lifestyle that we have been living since 2020. This includes changes to our daily lives such as preventive measures to avoid infection and working from home. The next normal is the post-pandemic world that we will be entering soon. This includes many of the same changes that we have been living with during the pandemic but also emphasizes the need to make more sustainable, long-term changes utilizing technology and different approaches to human interaction. The next normal also serves as an opportunity for us to reevaluate our lives and prioritize what's important to us, as well as make sure that we don't take anything for granted. It's a chance to make much-needed changes and create a better, more sustainable world for everyone.

In the next normal, our resilience will not only be tested by diseases such as COVID-19, Ebola, and Mpox. It will be an ever-changing period of adjustment to instability. Climate change is disrupting animal ecosystems and driving new viruses across species boundaries, potentially leading to further pandemics. We must also prepare for extreme weather events, social unrest, political upheaval, economic stagnation, and inequality—plus geopolitical power struggles. To survive in this environment demands not just preparedness but constant adaptability. Our ability to stay resilient in the face of such uncertainty will decide our fate.

The next normal is caused by interconnecting big and small crises and disruptions, which have a rippling and magnifying effect throughout the world that leads to years of instability. It's both a threat and an opportunity. Think of it as dealing with "everything everywhere all at once" in ways none of us has experienced. Yet, like the 2022 movie of the same name, we can learn to affect positive change by recognizing and acting upon the interconnectedness of our intent.

To start with, we need to put people back at the center of everything we do. That means creating an inclusive culture where everyone can thrive. Joe Loizzo, a Harvard-trained psychiatrist and Buddhist scholar, says this is a pivotal moment for business and society. We need to look at problems through a much wider lens so that changes are inclusive for workers at all skill levels and from all backgrounds. "Are we really helping people develop the capacity to sustain the complex, challenging lives we live while feeling grounded and being at ease?" he asks (Basiouny 2022).

The pandemic has shown us that employees are capable of great things under extreme stress, even when working remotely. This success has empowered workers, and they want to continue feeling a sense of value and contribution. We need to make sure our businesses are places where people can thrive.

If we could rise above the noisy confusion and dogma of the remote versus all in-office versus hybrid workplace debate, we would see that, regardless of the approach employers and leaders adopt, we need better-defined skills for managers and those who follow them to succeed together. Unless companies completely revert to their pre-pandemic work locations practices and adjust to the massive resignations of those who disapprove and the displeasure of those who remain, we will most certainly have a world in which video calls and on-site congregation coexist in some combination.

Why, how, and when that happens, and who participates, ought to be decided intentionally because it leads to the most compassionate and productive outcome, not because it's "just so" as the leader wants it to be. Because most managers today have some pre-pandemic experience with in-office leadership approaches, I'll focus my comments on skills needed for remote and hybrid work.

THE LEADER'S ROLE IN REMOTE AND HYBRID WORK

First and foremost, effective remote and hybrid managers had better be intentional about creating and maintaining team cohesion. When everyone isn't physically together in an office, it takes extra effort to ensure team members feel connected to one another and invested in the team's success. This starts with regular, clear communication from the manager about the team's goals, progress, and challenges. But it also requires ongoing opportunities for team members to interact socially and build relationships with one another.

Second, remote and hybrid managers need to be experts at using technology to facilitate communication and collaboration. With team members in different locations, or even just working remotely at different times, it's essential to have systems and tools in place that everyone can use to stay connected and work together effectively. This might include video call software for team meetings, project management tools to track assignments and deadlines, or instant messaging apps for quick questions and conversations.

Finally, remote and hybrid managers should be flexible and able to adjust their approach as the needs of their team change. What works well for a mostly remote team may not work as well when some team members start coming into the office more often. And as the pandemic continues to evolve, the manager's approach may need to change again. The key is to be open to new ideas and willing to experiment to find what works best for your team.

HIRING FOR THE NEXT NORMAL

When we hire supervisors and managers, it's important to make sure they have the aptitude and experience to get the most out of their people's work. My experience in management consulting taught me how to form teams with diverse skills and personalities and how to help them be productive under tight deadlines. I believe employers should look to professions that have similarly demanding expectations when it comes to hiring practices. In other words, the best managers will thoughtfully move their teams from forming, storming, and norming to performing quickly, repeatably, and pervasively.

First responders (police, firefighters, and emergency medical technicians), Peace Corps volunteers, military veterans, and community health workers are all examples of groups of people who work in high-stress and possibly low-resource circumstances where compassion for colleagues and those they serve is required to do their jobs well. Of course, the ultimate test of leading whole people wholeheartedly would be astronauts on a mission to Mars, once they exist. Wouldn't it be wonderful if researchers and scholars could unveil the hiring practices used by NASA, SpaceX, and Blue Origin, and codify them for use here on Earth now?

In Clayton C. Anderson's 2015 book *The Ordinary Spaceman: From Boyhood Dreams to Astronaut*, he shares his fifteen-year quest—with several rejections—to become an astronaut (Anderson 2015). Beyond his degrees in science and engineering, his pilot's and scuba licenses, and a stint as NASA's manager of the Emergency Operations Center, he looked for ways to make himself stand out.

As a college basketball referee, he argued, he had to make quick decisions and stick by them under a lot of pressure from people adversely affected by his rulings. In his final, successful interview to become an astronaut, he pointed out that he was from Nebraska, and NASA had never had an astronaut from that state. This type of whole-person preparedness approach—not necessarily the specific education and skills—stands out to me as someone who can handle any type of crisis they encounter.

PERFORMANCE UNDER CRISES

We also need to deeply probe and understand all job applicants' performance under crisis and have ways of assessing how their personality traits, working styles, and communication approaches support compassion, accountability, empowerment, and engagement under the worst of circumstances for them, their loved ones, colleagues, and subordinates.

The purveyors of popular assessment tools like Myers-Briggs Type Indicators, CliftonStrengths by Gallup, DiSC profile, Hogan assessment, and others must prove their databases and algorithms are tested under pandemic conditions, which would form the next normal's baseline, and can be interpreted for future crises.

CAREER GROWTH

The key to a successful remote or hybrid workforce is thoughtful management with a focus on career growth. This priority undoubtedly inspires and invigorates workers, even if they're thousands of miles away from one another. What we need are people who make informed and objective decisions about synchronous and asynchronous communication. Synchronous communications are scheduled, real-time interactions by phone, video, or in person. Asynchronous communication happens on your own time and doesn't need scheduling. Investing each other's time effectively could provide more time to focus on career growth.

Those who have already been hired need to be evaluated under job descriptions and expectations that make remote or hybrid work conditions explicit. Supervisors who hung over your shoulder and bugged you about tasks before the pandemic won't lead thriving remote or hybrid workforces. Instead, we need to focus on creating an environment that encourages career growth and development. This will ensure our workers are motivated and inspired, even when they're not in the office.

TO MEET OR NOT TO MEET?

In a December 1, 2021, *Harvard Business Review* article, "Remote Work Should Be (Mostly) Asynchronous," Steve Glaveski (2021) offers numerous recommendations for specific tools as well as a very important idea: You and your team need a single source of truth. This was a signature Lisa

Nibauer approach at OraSure that led to great success. It may be a shared Notion document (within which you can include calendars, pipelines of work, tables, and so on), a Google Doc, or another constantly synced cloud-based document where anything you're working on lives.

Ed Zitron is a fierce and articulate advocate for remote work and a writer for his own blog and *The Atlantic*. He believes in a single source of truth in sharing, "Honestly, there's something quite special about having a body of work that you've built together. Instead of simply talking every week about what you've done and what you want to do, you have a regular, documented feedback loop—no matter how physically far away you may be from each other" (Zitron 2022). Because OraSure's growth during the pandemic greatly outstripped its prior investment in this type of technology, we felt the pain of missing single sources of truth and crisp feedback loops until we all rallied behind the cause.

Christoph Riedl and Anita Woolley's research titled "Successful Remote Teams Communicate in Bursts," published in *HBR* on October 28, 2020, suggests that the most creative and productive virtual teams only communicate intermittently. They might even go days without talking to each other. But once they're in contact, they have messages and bits of code flying back and forth. This mode is called "burstiness." It's when collaboration is marked by a pattern of high energy and an abundance of creative ideas. To get to that place, you need to be communicating in real time. This idea of giving people independent time for their work and separate collaborative time for group work is at the heart of making remote collaboration effective.

Another key factor is focused attention without distractions. When people set aside time for uninterrupted work, they can find flow. They get absorbed in their tasks and enter a state of peak productivity. This is much different from the way most of us work, where we are constantly interrupted and never given the chance to focus. Scheduled quiet time gives people the opportunity to achieve focus and flow. At OraSure, we found the proliferation of meetings was the biggest enemy of flow and focus. We all need to be clearer about the need for every meeting as a start to decluttering our schedules.

If we want our remote team to be successful, we also need to plan our gatherings more purposefully. Synchronous meetings are essential to combating the "island" effect. As leaders, it's important to hear our employees' voices frequently and pay attention to their messaging in how they discuss their work. Leaders ought to bring their best listening selves to these gatherings.

MANAGEMENT IN THE NEXT NORMAL

In a predominantly remote future, the need for layer upon layer of bureaucracy in American work will be challenged by the rejection of the assumption that "management" is the only way to grow in a company. When a majority of employees are remote, a manager's mission is to sort the assets of an organization and utilize them to their fullest rather than a title that mostly means "I make sure you're working."

"A great manager can take a good worker and make them great or take an average worker and make them good," says

Zitron. It's an adjustment from seeing young, inexperienced people as "employees who must be tolerated until they're good" to seeing them as "early-stage investments who can be grown into something incredibly valuable" (Zitron 2021). That's always been true, and it's been exacerbated by the pandemic.

The internet has made the world a much smaller place, which has all sorts of implications for the way we work. One of the most significant is that it's no longer necessary to have someone physically present to keep people on task. This means that positions like mentors, sponsors, and coaches become more important as they can help workers get the most out of their abilities.

CALL FOR BETTER TOOLS

Zoom, Microsoft Teams, WebEx, and their ilk are examples of technologies that have to step up their game to better bridge the gap between remote and hybrid work. Too often, those who are gathered in traditional conference rooms and those participating individually from their home or somewhere else have markedly different experiences during video conferences.

There is a more egalitarian ethos when everyone is in a separate box on a video screen rather than two or more in a common box, especially when there's a distorted fisheye or long-lens shot of a near-empty conference room. Depending on personalities, communication style, and positional power, people tend to over- or under-participate when that happens. We need cameras, microphones, software, and internet connectivity that can reestablish an equitable presence in meetings.

Peter Fitzgerald, vice president of Global Partnerships, Platforms, and Ecosystems for Google, leads an organization to develop next-generation services for Google users. He knows we need better technology to access and participate in "any meeting, anywhere, on any device." It begins with companies providing necessary security on their devices—laptops, tablets, and smartphones—to permit employees to work flexibly. Companies also need to invest in huge flat-screen monitors, upgraded cameras, and audio systems for their meeting rooms.

"Then we'll also need technology to enable good meetings," he shared with me. "For example, enabling people to raise their hand digitally when you're in a larger group avoids the acoustical challenge of speaking up and overcoming background noises, particularly in large gatherings," he continued. Finally, he shared, "Over time, better meetings could be enabled by virtual reality. A breakthrough would enable three-dimensional presence, or copresence, as it's often called." Right now, the cost of widespread use of such technology is prohibitive. But when costs decline, he said, "We'll have the ability to have better conversations that overcome the current awkward hybrid-work challenges. There will be a lot of innovation here, and a lot of experimentation is going to be required."

Any company that wants to get the most out of its meetings should also consider using technology similar to Otter.ai, a

California-based technology company that develops speech-to-text transcription and translation applications using artificial intelligence and machine learning. Otter.ai shows captions for live speakers and generates written transcriptions, making meetings more meaningful. I spoke to Otter.ai's CEO and cofounder Sam Liang about how the software supports both audio and visual learning. He explained to me that seeing the transcript of a meeting can help people understand it better than just listening to it. "Searchability within transcripts is important," he said. "You can jump around and find relevant portions of discussions quickly."

With Otter.ai, there is no need to take notes because they are generated automatically. This can be helpful because it creates a transcript of the meeting that can be referenced later, allowing participants to focus on the discussion. In addition, people tend to speak more carefully when they know they are being recorded, which can help keep the discussion on track.

WHY RETURN TO THE OFFICE?

Before demanding employees return to the office, leaders are obliged to first consider a few key questions.

1. In what ways is my presence in the office for my benefit?
2. In what ways is my presence in the office for the benefit of those I serve?
3. What are the direct and indirect costs of synchronous meeting time? How do they compare for in-person and hybrid-working situations?

4. How do I think about the effectiveness of asynchronous communication?
5. What have I learned about avoiding crisis with preemptive communication during the pandemic?

If leaders act before carefully answering and evaluating these questions, they may find themselves under duress, having to explain why people need to be in the office when they could be working from home just as easily. With as many crises looming in the next normal, we don't need to add any more avoidable problems to the mix.

The recent wave of resignations isn't just people quitting their jobs. It's a mass rejection of the idea that burnout is an inevitable part of success and a reset of employees' life priorities. This shift presents a unique opportunity for leaders to embrace exploration and position their companies for a renaissance.

People are waking up to the possibility of decoupling jobs from geography that, along with a tight labor market, gives us the power to pursue our dreams. If we're focused on resignation, we're missing out on the chance to create something new and better. Empathy and support are key ingredients in successful exploration. By creating a brave and safe space for people to share their hopes and fears, we can help them find their way to a more fulfilling future.

Dear Steve...

———

"Here's what you've unknowingly taught me personally:

- Be intentional in everything I do.
- Live with purpose.
- Read, read, read.
- Be fearless in my DE&I journey.
- Work-life balance.
- Lead with integrity and be approachable.
- Mentorship is invaluable.

Also, thank you for your genuine support. It played a big part in our success."

CHAPTER 10

Through the Looking Glass

———

"[…] believe those who are seeking the truth; doubt those who find it; doubt everything, but don't doubt of yourself."

—ANDRÉ GIDE, FRENCH AUTHOR AND

NOBEL LAUREATE FOR LITERATURE

Chick Corea was one of the most influential and innovative musicians of our time. His unique style and approach to music inspired generations of musicians and helped bring piano music to new heights. Chick was a true pioneer, always exploring new territory and pushing the boundaries of his craft. He had a gift for communication, which allowed him to connect with listeners from all backgrounds and walks of life. Chick Corea was a true dragoman, appealing to listeners across genres and leading the way for others to follow in his musical footsteps. Thanks to him, the world is a more vibrant and exciting place for me. Sadly, he passed away during the pandemic in February 2021. I'll always cherish his music.

I played Chick Corea's "Spain" for my high school jazz ensemble audition and won awards for my contributions to the band. His 1978 album, *The Mad Hatter*, was a Billboard Top Jazz Album and is often on my playlist. It is a concept album inspired by Lewis Carroll's 1865 novel *Alice's Adventures in Wonderland*. I found the album especially helpful as a soundtrack to my pandemic experience as it helped me make sense of the many bizarre, senseless, distorted, and misfit elements of our world.

My OraSure story ends—for now—the way a cross-genre musical performance reflects the emotional journey I've been on. It's a mix of jazz, samba, and rock, with digital distortion all together with clarity about the paradoxes of my life. It's revealing and haunting, but also triumphant. As an elder in today's complicated world, I see great wisdom and potential for connection, even in the face of much adversity.

TRUTH-SEEKING BEGINS WITH CURIOSITY

Like many of us seeking truth, Alice's journey begins with curiosity. We're curious about the world around us and how it works. We're curious about new things and how we can learn about them. And, of course, we're curious about the white rabbit. This curiosity drives us to chase him down the rabbit hole and into a strange and unfamiliar world. But it also fuels our desire to find out more, to understand what we're seeing and hearing, and to uncover the truth. This same curiosity has led my journey from OraSure and continues to propel me forward.

On March 28, 2022, I sent my final MMM as an attempt to find some closure to my tenure at OraSure and offer perspective to my colleagues who would carry on.

I began writing Monday Motivational Messages on April 6, 2020, with deft editing from our Corporate Communications team. It seems appropriately symmetric and tidy that my last one would conclude two full years' worth of shared thoughts with you.

I've tried to use these MMMs as a platform when potentially controversial issues have come up related to social justice, public health, mental health, and other areas linked to our LIVE IT values, our DE&I and sustainability initiatives, and mentoring. I've also written opinion-editorial pieces and TANGram blog posts to amplify these topics for readers outside of our organization. I applaud those of you who provided me with feedback on any topic—whether you agreed with me or not. When you did so, I was delighted to send you a note back with gratitude.

When I took the CEO job in April 2018, I shared with our board that I intended to recruit, develop, and promote executives who were capable of succeeding me as CEO in three to five years. To do so, we needed to put the right people in the right leadership roles, empower them, and make them accountable. Our company's tremendous growth has created many opportunities for all of us to grow professionally and personally. That's the sweet part of a bittersweet farewell for me:

seeing all of you grow in your roles. I thank each of you for the opportunity to lead and mentor you.

So, what does my career transition mean to me? Here's what I've learned, so far…

—Have a sense of humor: As the sign on an old car parked precariously on the side of a less-traveled country road proclaims, "When one door closes, another one opens… Other than that, it's a pretty good car."

—There are old, funny-sounding words to describe it: "Coddiwomple [from the Old English]: to travel purposefully toward an as-yet-unknown destination."

—No one really believes I'm going to retire. So instead of pulling a "Tom Brady" and un-retiring in forty days, I'll call my next chapter a "pause" or "sabbatical," for now.

Through your feedback on my many MMMs, I've come to understand our common human nature: Many people are afraid to show their true selves to others because they worry they will be judged. However, most people are attracted to others who seem real and down-to-earth. So being vulnerable and open with others can make them more interested in you. Courageously admitting your weaknesses doesn't make you weaker; it makes you stronger in the long run.

Slowly, I'm surrounding those paradoxes and learning to address them. I hope you are too.

During my pause (however long it lasts), I'll be tackling these and other paradoxes. I want to learn better how to hold opposing ideas in my mind at the same time and still function. Some call this learning the genius of the "and" and overcoming the tyranny of the "or." I'll be working on merging these seeming opposites…

Creativity *and* discipline,

Innovation *and* execution,

Humility *and* audacity,

Freedom *and* responsibility.

This is the work of my life's next chapter. Wish me luck. It's going to be messy!

When the Caterpillar asks Alice, "Who are you?" Alice can barely stammer out a reply, "I—hardly know." I felt the quintessential vulnerability of an adolescent child whose growth and knowledge of self and the world changed so rapidly between 2020 and 2022 that a sense of identity becomes highly precarious, if not fleeting.

WHO AM I?

Just like Alice, I, too, have felt lost and uncertain of who I am in recent years. As the world around me morphed at an unprecedented rate, it was hard to keep up and hold on to any sense of stability. It often felt like everything I knew was being turned upside down. But unlike Alice, I have not been content to sit idly by and let Caterpillar have all the answers. I have been on a quest to find my own truth, which has required me to look beyond my career identities of CEO, or chairman, or founder, monikers that I had held for thirty-three collective years of my life.

This journey has been about cultivating my inner pastor and dragoman and finding new inspiration in combining them into a role that may be needed in the next normal in communities small or large. My journey has been a process of trial and error, experimentation, and discovery. Finally, it has also been a messy process of which I'm not proud as a neat freak. But with each step forward, I am getting closer to understanding who I am and my place in this new world, for which I am eternally grateful.

In the days after leaving OraSure, I was stumbling around in the dark. I was grateful for many things in my life, but the negative events had a greater impact on my brain than the positive ones. That happens because of something called negativity bias. We don't see things as they are. We see them through the lens of our own biases and assumptions. We filter out anything that doesn't fit with our view of the world, however inaccurately negative it may be, and that can make it hard to see what's really happening.

I needed to feel my sadness and anger, and did so. We're all wired to search for stories that feel complete, with a beginning, middle, and end. The stories that make the most sense to us are the ones that feel true and have a connection to our past. We're looking for stories that confirm what we already believe rather than changing our minds. This created a dilemma for me since the pandemic disconnected us from the past and was a fascinating story by itself.

We can all aim to listen to others carefully, to understand each other. This way of listening is crucial for treating others the way they want to be treated rather than just the way we want to be treated. That's the Platinum Rule. When we take the time to truly listen to others, we open up the possibility for true connection and mutual respect. Listening with the intention of understanding is a practice with innumerable upside, in both our personal and professional lives.

HEEDING ADVICE

I dug up a message I sent two weeks before I agreed to step down in December 2021. I was reflecting on the toll a second winter holiday season under COVID-19 had on each of us, the difficult year of Jill's recovery from her near-fatal fall, along with our remarkable OraSure journey to launch InteliSwab. Little did I know how prescient and self-referentially humble my advice would be.

> While joy and happy family times are often associated with this time of year, the holiday season may also usher in feelings of stress, anxiety, depression, and loneliness. Plus, colder weather and darker days— along with lingering isolation from the pandemic— aren't making it any better.

Here's how I'm coping with the stress while still anticipating the fun and joy: It's important to be grateful for the good things in your life, even if they seem small. You're not alone if you're feeling down or struggling with something. Lots of people go through tough times. Be kind to yourself and others, and try to turn negative emotions into positive ones. Staying connected with friends and family who make you happy can help as well as getting exercise and fresh air. Getting enough sunlight is also important for your mood. Finally, don't forget to take care of yourself by resting, meditating, praying, and doing things you enjoy. This will give you the energy you need to keep going.

The ironic timing of my advice reminded me of Alice's self-reflection: "She generally gave herself very good advice, though she very seldom followed it." I enjoyed my newfound spaciousness to reconnect more deeply with Jill, my children, grandchildren, mother, and close friends. I recalled the advice provided some thirty-five years ago by my mentor, Arthur Humphrey, who admonished me, "If you don't take care of yourself in your fifties and sixties, you'll pay for it in your eighties and nineties." He's now ninety-five and still clear-headed and loving. Taking care of oneself in midlife has certainly paid off for him. And I'm ever grateful for the reminder to do the same.

"GOOD" OR "BAD" IS REVEALED OVER TIME

Truth will always remain elusive to seekers, as the ancient Chinese parable 塞翁失馬 (Sāi Wēng Shī Mǎ or Sāi Wēng) explains (Sairam 2018).

An old Chinese farmer saved up small amounts of money over a year to buy a new horse. Just a day after the farmer bought the horse, it ran away. The farmer's neighbor expressed grief, but the farmer himself was calm. "I hope you can get over this bad news," said the neighbor. "Good news or bad news, can't say," replied the farmer.

The next day, the horse returned to the farmer's house by itself and brought another stray horse with it. "Cheer up, we're going to multiply our farm income. That's great news," said the farmer's son. "Good news or bad news, can't say," replied the farmer, and he carried on with his work.

A week later, the farmer took the first horse to his farm, and his son took the second horse to follow his father to work. On the way, the second horse pushed the boy down and ran away. The boy's leg was fractured badly. That evening back home, the farmer's wife groaned, "We will have to spend all our extra savings on our son's broken leg. What terrible news." Once again, the farmer replied: "Good news or bad news, can't say."

A month later, the farmer's king announced a war on the neighboring nation. Citing a lack of foot soldiers, the king ordered all able-bodied men in the nation to get drafted into the military without excuses. The farmer's son was spared because of his broken leg. Later, the inexperienced soldiers got slaughtered in the war. "You are lucky your son did not get drafted. Mine returned with severe injuries. Many have been handicapped or killed," complained the farmer's best friend. Unabashed, the farmer responded: "Good news or bad news, can't say."

So, what lesson can we learn from the farmer? In life, it's impossible to predict whether an event will turn out ultimately to be good or bad. The best we can do is be present, openhearted and curious, and learn. For me, that means living, loving, and leading wholeheartedly. It's the motto of my life's work.

SEEKING *UBUNTU*

When I learned more about the late great South African bishop and human rights activist Desmond Tutu, I was amazed by his philosophy of *ubuntu*. This way of life, originating from Southern Africa, encompasses all our aspirations about how to live life well, together. We feel it when we connect with other people and share a sense of humanity, when we listen deeply and experience an emotional bond, and when we treat ourselves and other people with the dignity they deserve. The February 8, 2022, edition of the Center for Action and Contemplation newsletter titled "We Are One and Many: Members of One Diverse Family" struck home to me.

Tutu's granddaughter, Mungi Ngomane, is an author and activist who shared, "In my family, we were brought up to understand that a person who has *ubuntu* is one whose life is worth emulating. The bedrock of the philosophy is respect, for yourself and others. So, if you're able to see other people, even strangers, as fully human you will never be able to treat them as disposable or without worth" (CAC 2022).

I've found prayer and meditation help me align with *ubuntu*, the expansive universe, and my God, as well as the connection to every person I ever have and ever will encounter. By living with this philosophy, we can create a world that is more connected, compassionate, and respectful.

As I've continued to meditate, I've learned to enter more directly into a quiet, contemplative state of mind. Gradually, I've become more familiar with the inner landscape of my newly awakened heart. As my heart is allowed to rest in meditative awareness repetitively, it slowly discovers its center of gravity in the hidden depths of God and unconditional love.

I can understand what Ngomane is saying when she mentions that we are placed in a network of relationships with the divine, other humans, and the rest of creation. We are meant to live as members of one big family, showing off rich diversity within our different cultures, races, and backgrounds. And it is precisely because we are so diverse that we need to be interdependent.

AMBIGUITY AND THE TENSION OF OPPOSITES

In his book *Tuesdays with Morrie*, Mitch Albom discusses the importance of learning to deal with opposing concepts and scenarios (1997). He describes it as a tension of opposites, like a pull on a rubber band, and argues that most of us live somewhere in the middle. This tension is important because it requires a level of comfort with ambiguity.

In the next normal, we will be faced with many decisions that must take into account seemingly opposite forces. For example, we must weigh the personal freedom to forego masks or get vaccinated against the need to protect public health. Neither I nor public policymakers can be static in our analysis of this void because, ultimately, we all need to make sound, timely decisions that affect people's lives and livelihoods. What's personal is also universal. We must learn to deal with the tension of opposites to make the best decisions for ourselves and others.

There are many examples of political, economic, and technological opposites that we, as a global community, need to resolve. I believe effective problem-solving on these big issues, and smaller ones, will only happen when we bridge opposites with "and," instead of debating them as the false choices of "or." Here are a few at the top of my mind:

- Capitalism *and* wealth inequality.
- Criminal justice reform *and* public safety.
- Consumption *and* sustainability.
- Mobility *and* greenhouse gas reduction.
- Artificial intelligence *and* job creation.
- National interests *and* global community.

We all need to get comfortable with ambiguity and embrace the tension of opposites. For my part, I'll be working to hold the discomfort of these paradoxes *and* translate them into possible solutions in ways that bring people together instead of further polarizing them. I believe that's the best way to provide more effective leadership and opportunity for everyone.

It can be helpful to think about opposite qualities in terms of tension. Tensions of opposites can reveal something meaningful about our nature, the tension between being capable and lost, smiling and struggling, kind and able to have boundaries, vulnerable and powerful, successful and traumatized, extrovert and alone, valued and flawed, introvert and engaging, loving and questioning.

Each of these paired words can be represented by a circle. The overlap between the circles reveals something about our human nature. As I began to reset my identity, I noticed there was near complete overlap between each word pair for me. That showed me that at any given moment, both descriptions could be true about me. Recalling the meaning of each word through life experiences without shame or judgment permits me to feel more fully alive.

COPING WITH BURNOUT

I dealt with the burnout I felt during my final three months at OraSure. In their book *Burnout*, authors Amelia and Emily Nagoski say people everywhere are "overwhelmed and exhausted and still feeling like they ought to be doing more" (2019). According to the Maslach Burnout Inventory—a psychological assessment with twenty-two factors describing job burnout—three factors lead to this condition: emotional exhaustion, depersonalization, and a diminished sense of personal accomplishment. And once burnout sets in, there are consequences to emotional and physical health, including heart disease, depression, weight gain, and chronic pain. I experienced all three burnout factors and began to see their inevitable effects on me.

One way I coped with my burnout was by talking to other people who had experienced it. In particular, I found it helpful to talk to people who had gone through burnout and come out on the other side. Hearing their stories and advice was reassuring and gave me hope that I would be able to get through my own experience. If you're dealing with burnout, I encourage you to reach out to someone who has been there before. Talking to someone who understands what you're going through can make a world of difference.

In today's world, it's more important than ever to take care of your mental health. With the pandemic causing increased levels of anxiety and depression, it's crucial to find ways to cope. I'm lucky to have had access to therapists, coaches, and spiritual guides who have helped me through some tough times. Meditation has become a key part of my morning routine, and I credit Modern Elder Academy in Baja California Sur, Mexico, for helping me get started on this path. If you're struggling, don't be afraid to reach out for help. It could make all the difference in your life.

BECOMING A MODERN ELDER

In his book *Wisdom@Work*, Chip Conley talks about his journey to become a modern elder (2018). He wants workplaces to be more like an "intergenerational potluck," where everyone brings something to the table. He notes that "power is moving to younger people in the business world and organizations because of our increasing reliance on DQ or digital intelligence." He also noted that some studies show power is ten years younger today than it was twenty years ago. This means there is a new twenty-year irrelevancy gap for people in midlife and beyond.

How can we take advantage of the differences between younger and older people? Instead of expecting young leaders to have all the same skills that older people have, we need to figure out how to share knowledge between generations. This way, everyone can learn from each other and create opportunities for everyone involved.

Wisdom and knowledge are different. Wisdom is not just about having a lot of knowledge. It's about understanding what is important and applying it in a way that is both helpful and humane. Computers can't do this. So, even though technology is improving quickly, we still need wisdom to make sense of everything around us.

Chip created a role for himself when he first joined Airbnb. He was a combination of mentor and intern, which he calls a "mentern." This means he would help other people learn and grow at the company but also learn new things himself. He thinks the traditional way of thinking—that wisdom only flows from older to younger people—is outdated. Nowadays, wisdom can flow in both directions, so he intends on being a modern elder and train legions of us of a certain age to join him.

FINALE

I'm not sure what Alice's ultimate fate was—Lewis Carroll left that mysterious—but I'm guessing she's doing pretty well for herself. She's matured, become a queen, and seems to have mastered her inner and outer game. She's learned to accept the madness and actively challenge the nonsense. And at the end of the story, she's still curious and resolute. I'd like to believe she's living her dream and loving it.

As for me, I leave you most assuredly knowing that I better understand my existence and the perspective my wild journey has provided me. I remain a seeker of truth with unending curiosity and renewed resolve. I'm engulfed in my dream of living, loving, and leading wholeheartedly wherever my journey takes me from here.

Acknowledgments

———

I have tremendous gratitude for many people who showed interest and provided support to me as a first-time author. When I left OraSure Technologies Inc. on March 31, 2022, part of me wanted to put the entire experience behind me and fade softly into everlasting peace. I didn't want to revisit the pain and agony of the pandemic and my departure. Then, I realized I could be a catalyst for stories that need to be told. To do so, I'd need a lot of encouragement and tough love from my community.

I covered the many trials and tribulations Jill and I faced in previous pages. So naturally, she deserves the first mention. As newlyweds, our relationship was tested mightily and often throughout the OraSure and pandemic experiences. Once we learned to grab the mirror and put away the projector when in our respective darkness, we figured out ways to better cocreate our life together from the quarantine and onward.

To someone who's shared a lifetime of loving kindness, I thank my mother, Helen, for inspiring me from childhood to adulthood. In the years leading up to 2020, she began sharing her life's story beginning in war-torn China in the 1940s to her immigration to and assimilation with America. Hers is quite a journey in its own right. I'm cheering for her to pick up the author's pen too.

My children give me hope for the future with their compassion and empathy. Since the pandemic began, my son and I have reconciled our relationship by finding common ground, one daughter presented me with two grandchildren, and the other graduated from university and entered the job market. What more could a father want for his children than to have them approach their worlds with hope, dedication, and courage while being loving people in their tribes and communities?

To all of the people whose stories I share in my book, named or unnamed—I am grateful for your trust, perspective, and honesty. I am in awe of your courage for opening up to me. It has been an honor to be entrusted with your stories, and I want you to know they are always safe with me. You all inspire me every day with your strength and bravery. You are my heroes!

I'd also like to thank Eric Koester, John Saunders, Brian Bies, Shanna Heath, Venus Bradley, Sherman Morrison, Chandra Elaine Spurlock, Chuck Oexmann, George Thorne, Emily VanderBent, and their teams I've had the honor to work with at the Book Creators Thought Leaders and New Degree Press. You've provided me the compass to seek my true north in this book-writing quest.

I would also like to extend a huge thank you to my editors—Zack Marcum, Ken Cain, Pavita Singh, Kayla LeFevre, and Nadara Merrill. I am grateful for your support in protecting my vision for this book and partnering with me on the chapters to bring it to life. Your encouragement pushed me to explore more, allowing me to tell a story that truly needed to be told. Additionally, the laughter and smiles we shared during our conversations were greatly appreciated as they reenergized my spirit and kept me moving forward.

I am immensely thankful to all those who have believed in my writing and provided me with necessary encouragement and candor. I would also like to express my gratitude to everyone who offered feedback on the initial drafts of this book—your help has been instrumental in making it what it is today. A special thanks to those who preordered my book. Your support has been overwhelming and reassuring. Your kindness and care prove that I am surrounded by an amazing community of people.

Val Adams

Peggy Agouris

Mark Andino

Cousin Angie

Anonymous

Manuel Thomas Aparicio

Ronchi

Esther Baldwin

Tony Bartolomeo

Mark Bastek

Cynthia Baum-Baicker

James Beenders

Jody Berry

Koen Beyers

Kenneth Blank

Neil Bodick

David Bookspan

Elwood Boykin

Colleen Bracken

Merry Broderick Woods

Patti Carabba

Craig Carnaroli

Dave Carver

Monica Cawvey Gallagher

Farland Chang
Catherine Chen
Jill Chernekoff
Art Chernekoff
Steven Chernekoff
Lorrayne Chu
Mark Clymer
Julie Cohen
Danielle Cohn
Sheri Collins
Linda Conlin
Charles Cooney
Lesley Corbin
Beth Covin
Tara Crawford Parks
Nicole Crenshaw
Jennifer Cunningham
Brian Curley
Eric Darr
Karen DeLone
Mark DiNardo
Dale Dirks
Steve Doberstein
Thomas Donley
Benjamin Doranz
Brian Duke
Eric Dzwonczyk
Michael Eckstut
Mohamed El-Aasser
Marla Emery
JoAnne Epps
Maria Esposito

Timothy Fallon
Jack Ferguson
June Fields
Francesca Fifis
Richard Findlay
Dory Ellen Fish
Beth Anne Fisher
Joseph A. Fitzpatrick, Jr.
Vincent Forlenza
Zachary Fowler
Allan Frank
Debra Fraser-Howze
Michelle Freeman
Robert S. Frisch
Marta Boulos Gabriel
Jessica Gage
Agnieszka (Aggie) Gallagher
Mitch Gershenfeld
Cathie Gillard
Global Coaching Alliance
LLC
Julie Goonewardene
Bonnie Grant
Alan Greenberger
Robert Greene
Evan Gutoff
William Hamilton
Maurice T Hampton
John Hanger
Lisa Popper Harris
Joseph Helble
Gerri Henwood

Hilda Herceg
Thomas Hess
Bill Hinchey
Karl Hofmann
Michael Holscher
Jack Horst
Ali Houshmand
Lee Huang
Arthur Humphrey
Diane White Husic
Victor Hwang
Marianne Intoccia
Alan Jacobson
Laurie Jantz
Immanuel Karuppumanil
  John
Phil Johnson
Corinne Kavounas
Yoshihiro Kawano
Christopher Keenan
Mark Kehoe
Patrick Kelley
David Kenney
Kat and Curtis Knecht
James Knox, Jr
Amy Koch
Eric Koester
Bob Kothari
Lisa Kramer
Kenneth Kring
Stephen Kusen
Matthew Lambert

Laura LaRosa
Tiffany Lawson
Clare Leinweber
Chase Lenfest
Julie Lenzer
Andrew Liang
Elaine and Calvin Liang
Horace Liang
Jeff Libson
Alex Liu
Megan Lott
David Lucas
Jeffrey Mack
Anthony Maher
Sue Manix
Phyllis Mann
Jennifer Mann
Michele Marcolongo
Leslie Mazza
Robert McGrath
Sylvia Watts McKinney
Nancy McLane
William J. Meagher, Jr.
Robert Mitchell
Christopher Molineaux
Thomas Morr
Don Morris
Curt Myers
Drake Nakaishi
Lisa Nibauer
Susan Noack (Atkinson)
Anne O'Callaghan

Dr. Henry Odi

Mike O'Rourke

Daniel Ou-Yang

J. David Owens

Douglas Parulis

Nihal Patel

Michael Patterson

Scott Peterman

James Peworchik

Jonathan Phillips

Bud Phillips

Due Quach

Krishnan Rajagopalan

Gillian Rajsic

Brian Regan

Todd Reinert

Cheryl Rice

Tyler Ridgeway

Geoffrey M. Roche

Jose Luis Rosado

Lauren Ryder

Brett Saks

Chris Satullo

John Saunders

Wei Scaltrito

Anne Schoemaker

Robert Schuck

Brendan See

Stuart Segal

Jay H. Shah

Shannon Shannon

Barry Sharp

Stan Silverman

Geoffrey Slaff

Abby Smith

Mark Smith

Heseung Ann Song

Jorge Soto

Adrian Stanley

Michael Steelman

Harvey Stenger

Daniel Stern

Eric Stern

Mary C. Stout, RN (retired)

Randall Sweet

Wesley Sweet

Helen Tang

Dave and Michelle Tang

Charlene Tappan

David Thornburgh

Ron Ticho

Andy Toy

Anthony Trentalange

Stephen Tullman

Richard Uhlig

Ryan Unger

Richard Vague

Vanessa Vankerckhoven

Maribel Wadsworth

Xiao-Wei Wang

Michael Wang

Keith Wang

Brent Ward

Kris Ward

Maximillion A.J. Wells III   Karen Wu Audi

Christopher White   Ken Yang

Jeremiah White   Susan Yee

Susan Wild   Jessica Young

Tiffany Wilson   Steve Zarrilli

James and Amy Wimer   Xinjin Zhao

Jason Wingard   Joseph Zickel

Kenneth Wong   Michael Zisman

Christina Wong   Jo-Ann Zoll

For anyone and everyone journeying out of your versions of darkness, here's the gratitude I shared in my journal the weeks after decompressing from OraSure:

> Thank you to my God for giving me a strong mind and fierce will that guide me through so many experiences. I'm grateful for your persistence and the decisions you have helped me make. It's now time for a new perspective; one of being, accepting, and openness. Rather than worrying endlessly about what's past or future, I will focus on the present moment.

> I am also thankful for those who have wounded me—their slights, transgressions, and cruelty have enabled me to become more aware of my past and learn from it. When I think of them now, I strive to observe them without attachment. This distance helps me recognize how much I have grown from these difficult experiences.

> I want to also extend my love and gratitude to the shy, awkward, kid of color within me who visits me

often. I know you are filled with insecurities and fears, but please remember you are enough as you are and life will be grand. Release negativity from your mind, body, and soul. There is much you can offer to this world.

Finally, thank you to those who have supported me throughout my life with unconditional love, patience, wisdom, and presence. I often take these people for granted; however, in moments of clarity, I recognize the immense value their love brings into my life.

About the Author

―――――

Featured as a "Renaissance Man" by *William and Mary Alumni Magazine* in 2022, Steve Tang has been a respected business, civic, and thought leader for many years. In his forty-year career, he has held the titles of chairman of the board, chief executive officer, and founder/owner for thirty-three combined years. His op-ed pieces have been published in *The Wall Street Journal*, *The Hill*, *Philadelphia Inquirer*, and *Morning Call* (Allentown, Pennsylvania). He is a frequent speaker and commentator on leadership, business, public policy, public health, innovation, and entrepreneurship.

Dr. Tang was president and CEO of OraSure Technologies, Inc. from 2018 to 2022. During this period, the company delivered record revenue growth and the largest expansion of innovative products, employees, and facilities in its thirty-five-year history. Its InteliSwab COVID-19 Rapid Test is recognized by Oprah Winfrey's company as the "easiest home COVID-19 test to use." OraSure is empowering the global community to improve health and wellness by providing access to accurate essential information. Dr. Tang previously served as OraSure's chairman of the board of directors (2016 through 2018) and was first elected to the board in 2011.

From 2008 to 2018, Dr. Tang served as president and CEO of the University City Science Center, the nation's first and largest urban research park in Philadelphia. During that decade, he initiated, led, and implemented a strategic plan designed to transform the Science Center from a traditional real-estate-focused research park to an innovation and workforce development powerhouse. From 2005 through 2008, he was a senior executive with Olympus America at the helm of its Life Science Group of businesses. Before that, he was an energy technology entrepreneur and a senior executive at two leading global management consulting firms.

Dr. Tang was reappointed to the National Advisory Council on Innovation and Entrepreneurship (NACIE) in 2016 and served as NACIE co-chair through 2018. Previously, he served on the US Department of Commerce's Innovation Advisory Board, from 2011 through 2012.

Along with Pennsylvania's governor, from 2015 through 2018, he co-chaired the Team Pennsylvania Foundation, which bridges the gap between state government and the private sector. He also served from 2014 through 2016 as chairman of the board of the Committee of Seventy—an independent, nonpartisan advocate for better government in Philadelphia that works to achieve clean and effective government, better elections, and informed and engaged citizens. He was the first person of color elected to chair both of these organizations.

Dr. Tang has served several multiyear stints on advisory and fiduciary boards for the College of William and Mary in Virginia, Lehigh University, Seton Hall University, Thomas Jefferson University, Temple University, University of the Sciences, Harrisburg University, the Greater Philadelphia Chamber of Commerce, and Life Science Pennsylvania.

He has received numerous honors and awards, including the 2022 Lehigh University Distinguished Alumni Award for Outstanding Entrepreneurship, the 2021 Seventh Annual Globy Award for Corporate Leadership from Global Philadelphia Association, the 2021 Lehigh Valley Business' Healthcare Power 30 List member, the 2021 Pennsylvania Healthcare Power 100 from City and State Pennsylvania, the 2021 Spirit of Innovation Award (on behalf of OraSure) from the National Museum of Industrial History, the 2018 Leadership Award from the Association of University Research Parks, the 2018 Dennis Clark Solas Award from the Welcoming Center for New Pennsylvanians, Philadelphia Magazine's 2017 100 Most Influential Philadelphians (#28), City and State Pennsylvania's 2017 50 Over Fifty, Philadelphia Business Journal's 2017 Power 100, Rad-Girls.com's 2016 Rad Guy of the Year, and was named one of Philadelphia Business Journal's 2015 Most Admired Chief Executive Officers.

Dr. Tang earned a PhD and MS in Chemical Engineering from Lehigh University, an MBA from the Wharton School of Business at the University of Pennsylvania, and a BS in Chemistry from the College of William and Mary. He also has been awarded honorary Doctor of Humane Letters degrees from Philadelphia University (a.k.a. Thomas

Jefferson University) and Philadelphia's Wagner Free Institute of Science.

Steve was born in Madison, Wisconsin, and raised in Wilmington, Delaware, and then Beaumont, Texas, and then back to Delaware, where he attended public schools. He lived and raised his family in the Lehigh Valley, Pennsylvania, from 1982 through 2013. He is married to Jill Chernekoff, an executive leadership development coach and former Emmy Award-winning Philadelphia television reporter and news anchor. He is the father of three adult children and two grandchildren. Steve and Jill make their home in Bala Cynwyd, Pennsylvania.

You can reach Steve through his website: www.Tang.ceo.

Appendix

———

Introduction

Jankowicz, Mia. 2021. "The Guy Driving Suez Canal Excavator Said He Had 3 Hours of Sleep a Night and Has Been Paid No Overtime." *Business Insider.* April 8, 2021. https://www. businessinsider.co.za/suez-excavator-driver-worked-21-hour-days-hasnt-got-overtime-2021-4.

Sukheja, Bhavya. 2021. "Driver of Suez Canal Excavator Hasn't Been Paid His Overtime, Didn't Like Becoming a Meme." *Republic World.* April 9, 2021. https://www.republicworld.com/ world-news/middle-east/driver-of-suez-canal-excavator-hasnt-been-paid-his-overtime-didnt-like-becoming-a-meme.html.

Prologue

Roberts, Kayleigh. "Barack Obama Says Michelle Obama Never Fully Forgave Him for Running for President after She Initially Said No." *Marie Claire Magazine.* November 26, 2020. https:// www.marieclaire.com/celebrity/a34797897/barack-obama-says-michelle-obama-never-forgave-him-for-running-for-president/.

Chapter 1

McNeil, Donald G. 2021. "Rapid H.I.V. Home Test Wins Federal Approval." *The New York Times*. July 3, 2012. https://www.nytimes.com/2012/07/04/health/oraquick-at-home-hiv-test-wins-fda-approval.html.

Weinberger, Sharon. 2014. "100-Year Starship: Mae Jemison reaches for the stars." *BBC*. November 18, 2014. https://www.bbc.com/future/article/20120518-reaching-for-the-stars.

Zhao, Xinjin. 2020. "Coronavirus Crisis in China" *LinkedIn Pulse* (blog). January 30, 2020. https://www.linkedin.com/pulse/coronavirus-crisis-china-xinjin-zhao/.

Chapter 2

Engbrecht, Shawn. 2018. *Invisible Leadership: Transforming Risk into Opportunity*. Wichita, Kansas: Prime Concepts Group Press.

Grant, Adam Forrest. 2021. *Think Again: The Power of Knowing What You Don't Want*. New York: Penguin Random House.

Kidd, Sue Monk. 1990. *When the Heart Waits: Spiritual Direction for Life's Sacred Questions*. San Francisco: Harper.

Lord, Phil, and Christopher Miller. 2014. *The LEGO Movie*. Warner Brothers. 1 hr. 40 mins. https://www.warnerbros.com/movies/lego-movie.

Chapter 3

McCann, Erin. 2021. "Astronauts Talk about What Life Is Like After Space." *Ranker*. September 23, 2021. https://www.ranker.com/list/astronauts-returning-to-earth-after-space/erin-mccann.

Chapter 4

Ancona, Deborah, Michele Williams, and Gisele Gerlach. 2020. "The Overlooked Key to Leading through Chaos." *MIT Sloan Management Review*. September 8, 2020. https://sloanreview.mit.edu/article/the-overlooked-key-to-leading-through-chaos/.

George, Bill, and Zach Clayton. 2022. *True North: Leading Authentically in Today's Workplace*. Hoboken, New Jersey: John Wiley and Sons, Inc.

George, Bill and Peter Sims. 2007. *True North: Discover Your Authentic Leadership*. New York: Jossey-Bass.

Hoover, Margaret. 2022. "Adam Grant." *Public Broadcasting Service*. Streamed live on August 10, 2022. PBS video. 26 mins. https://www.pbs.org/wnet/firing-line/video/adam-grant-ya6blk/.

Meyer, Claire. 2020. "McChrystal: Focus on Empowering Frontline Decision-Makers." *ASIS Homepage*. September 24, 2020. https://www.asisonline.org/security-management-magazine/

articles/2020/gsx-show-daily-2020/McChrystal-focus-on-Empowering-Frontline-Decision-Makers/.

Chapter 5

Brown, Brené. 2012. *Daring Greatly*. New York: Avery.

Cain, Susan. 2022. *Bittersweet: How Sorrow and Longing Make Us Whole*. New York: Crown Publishing Group.

Renz, Eddie. 2021. "Collective Effervescence Archives." *iteach*. September 14, 2021. https://www.iteach.net/blog/category/collective-effervescence/.

Tulshyan, Ruchika. 2013. "Condoleezza Rice—Former Secretary of State." *Little PINK Book*. August 29, 2013. https://littlepinkbook.com/condoleezza-rice-former-secretary-of-state/.

Chapter 6

George, Bill, and Jay Lorsch. 2014. "How to Outsmart Activist Investors." *Harvard Business Review*. November 5, 2014. https://hbr.org/2014/05/how-to-outsmart-activist-investors.

Stewart, James B. 2015. "Fired Founder Watches Men's Wearhouse Struggle." *News-Journal*. November 29, 2015. https://www.news-journal.com/news/business/fired-founder-watches-mens-wearhouse-struggle/article_6d9278d5-4a97-5321-9ff0-312b9a551cbb.html.

Chapter 7

Smith, Doug C. 1999. *Being a Wounded Healer: How to Heal Ourselves While We Are Healing Others*. Madison, Wisconsin: Psycho-Spiritual Publications.

Chapter 8

Rothbard, Nancy, and David Pottruck. 2022. "Integrators and Segmentors: Managing Remote Workers." *Wharton Executive Education*. February 25, 2022. https://executiveeducation.wharton.upenn.edu/thought-leadership/wharton-at-work/2020/08/managing-remote-workers/.

Sinek, Simon. 2020. "Simon Sinek: How Leaders Inspire Even in a Time of Crisis | Inc." Inc. June 24, 2020. 59 mins. https://www.youtube.com/watch?v=uhZdbL-ekW8.

Taleb, Nassim Nicholas. 2016. *Antifragile: Things That Gain from Disorder*. New York: Random House.

The Conference Board. 2022. *C-Suite Outlook 2022: Reset and Reimagine*. New York: The Conference Board.

Wallace-Wells, David. 2022. "Endemic COVID-19 Looks Pretty Brutal." *The New York Times*. July 20, 2022. https://www.nytimes.com/2022/07/20/opinion/covid-19-deaths-vaccines-endemic.html.

Chapter 9

Anderson, Clayton C. 2015. *Ordinary Spaceman: From Boyhood Dreams to Astronaut.* Lincoln, Nebraska: University of Nebraska Press.

Basiouny, Angie. 2022. "Finding Balance in a Post-Pandemic Workplace." *Knowledge at Wharton.* June 19, 2022. https://knowledge.wharton.upenn.edu/article/finding-balance-in-a-post-pandemic-workplace/.

Glaveski, Steve. 2021. "Remote Work Should Be (Mostly) Asynchronous." *Harvard Business Review.* December 1, 2021. https://hbr.org/2021/12/remote-work-should-be-mostly-asynchronous.

Riedl, Christoph, and Anita Williams Woolley. 2021. "Successful Remote Teams Communicate in Bursts." *Harvard Business Review.* August 17, 2021. https://hbr.org/2020/10/successful-remote-teams-communicate-in-bursts.

Zitron, Ed. 2021. "Say Goodbye to Your Manager." *The Atlantic.* September 17, 2021. https://www.theatlantic.com/ideas/archive/2021/09/manager-work-life-changes/620096/.

Zitron, Ed. 2022. "How to Mentor Young Workers in a Remote World." *The Atlantic.* January 14, 2022. https://www.theatlantic.com/ideas/archive/2022/01/good-management-mentorship-remote-world/621219/.

Chapter 10

Albom, Mitch. 1997. *Tuesdays with Morrie: An Old Man, a Young Man, and Life's Greatest Lesson*. New York: Doubleday.

Anonymous. 2022. "Daily Meditation: Members of One Diverse Family." *Center for Action and Contemplation*. February 8, 2022. https://cac.org/daily-meditations/members-of-one-diverse-family-2022-02-08/.

Conley, Chip. 2018. *Wisdom@Work: The Making of a Modern Elder*. Sydney, Australia: Currency Press.

Nagoski, Emily, and Amelia Nagoski. 2019. *Burnout: The Secret to Solving the Stress Cycle*. New York: Ballantine Books.

Sairam, Disnesh. 2018. "The Farmer and His Horse: What Is the Meaning of Life?" *LinkedIn Pulse* (blog). February 21, 2018. https://www.linkedin.com/pulse/farmer-his-horse-what-meaning-life-dinesh-sairam/.